How AI Will Destroy Humanity
Part II

Elysia Duke

ISBN-13: 979-8-28194-097-9

DEDICATION

I dedicate my book to individuals who put in hard work and advocate for their jobs to ensure durable quality of products and services. The world will be inaccurate if AI completely takes over.

"The magic is only in what books say, how they stitched the patches of the universe together into one garment for us."
— *Ray Bradbury, Fahrenheit 451*

"Who controls the past controls the future. Who controls the present controls the past."
— *George Orwell, 1984*

"The future belongs to those who believe in the beauty of their dreams."
— *Eleanor Roosevelt*

CONTENTS

ACKNOWLEDGMENTS

There have been developments in AI since my last book and maybe some topics that I forgot. This book uses cited research from reliable sources. Locations mentioned in the book were fact-checked using Google Street View.

1 DEVELOPMENTS SINCE LAST BOOK

There have been some developments in artificial intelligence (AI) that are continuously evolving and new ideas are infinite. There would be a finite number of skilled trades left, which would be outsourced to AI. As mentioned in the previous book, AI is considered defective and disastrous.

AI in employment will worsen as more Baby Boomers retire from skilled trades and younger workers are not educated on how specific tasks work. There are also a lot of people who do not want to do any work onsite at all and would just "draw a check." According to Howarth (2025), 300 million jobs may be lost to AI by 2025.[1] Worse, 14% of all workers have been displaced by AI.[2] Automating half of the world's current tasks could take another 20 years.[3] Workers aged 18 to 24 are 129% more likely than those over 65 to be concerned that AI may render their jobs obsolete.[4]

Technology is a continual element striking the future viewpoint for several occupations, and AI is a relatively new technology type with possible ramifications, according to the US Bureau of Labor Statistics (2025).[5] Over the 2023-33 job projection period, AI is predicted to have the greatest impact on jobs whose basic functions are easily copied by Generative AI in its present form.[6] Other occupations, which includes those in the architectural, business, computer, engineering, finance, and legal occupational categories, are also possibly vulnerable to AI-related effects, albeit their employment trajectories are unknown.[7] Several computer-related jobs employ AI in their daily operations.[8] Programming is one of several job functions where AI may supplement human efforts and boost efficiency.[9] AI may assist software engineers in writing,

---

[1] Howarth, Josh. "60+ Stats on AI Replacing Jobs (2025)." Exploding Topics, April 3, 2025. https://explodingtopics.com/blog/ai-replacing-jobs.
[2] Ibid.
[3] Ibid.
[4] Ibid.
[5] U.S. Bureau of Labor Statistics. "Ai Impacts in BLS Employment Projections." U.S. Bureau of Labor Statistics, March 11, 2025. https://www.bls.gov/opub/ted/2025/ai-impacts-in-bls-employment-projections.htm.

[6] Ibid.
[7] Ibid.
[8] Ibid.
[9] Ibid.

testing, and documenting code, improving information quality, and developing user narratives that explain how a software attribute will supply value.[10] Nevertheless, AI might increase the computer employment demand by requiring software originators to create AI-based business results and manage AI systems, as well as database architects and administrators to construct and manage increasing complex data infrastructure.[11]

According to Joshi (2025), AI is altering the global economy, with significant ramifications for the job market.[12] AI technologies are displacing certain vocations while also opening up new chances in emerging industries.[13] Understanding the full magnitude of these developments is critical for governments, organizations, and employees alike.[14]

According to Kelly (2025), bookkeeping, financial modeling, and basic data analysis are quite vulnerable.[15] Paralegal work, contract drafting, and legal research are excellent targets for AI solutions like Harvey and CoCounsel, which automate document analysis with 90% accuracy.[16] Senior legal strategy and courtroom arguments will, however, take longer due to human judgment requirements.[17] Graphic design, copywriting, and basic journalism are being disrupted by tools like DALL-E and GPT-derived systems that generate material on a large scale.[18] AI has a twofold benefit in software development, engineering, and data science: it increases efficiency while also automating common coding and design activities.[19] Complex innovation, such as breakthrough research and development, will continue to be driven by humans for the foreseeable future.[20] Diagnostic AI and robotic surgery are improving, but empathy-driven professions such as nursing, therapy, and social work are more difficult to automate.[21] Teaching, particularly in complex subjects like as philosophy or early education, as well as high-level managerial positions, require emotional intelligence and adaptability, which AI struggles to imitate.[22]

AI in the trucking industry is stated to reduce the number of accidents, but Robo-Trucker should not be trusted. Many attorneys across the country have launched instructions on their individual websites about accidents that may be caused by an AI-powered vehicle or statements on accident reduction. According to Sloan (2024), a driverless semi-truck rolled over roughly 300 feet through a residential neighborhood in

---

[10] Ibid.

[11] Ibid.

[12] Joshi, Satyadhar. "Generative AI: Mitigating Workforce and Economic Disruptions While Strategizing Policy Responses for Governments and Companies." *International Journal of Advanced Research in Science, Communication and Technology* 5, no. 1 (February 12, 2025): p. 480. https://doi.org/10.48175/ijarsct-23260.

[13] Ibid.

[14] Ibid.

[15] Kelly, Jack. "The Jobs That Will Fall First as AI Takes over the Workplace." Forbes, April 25, 2025. https://www.forbes.com/sites/jackkelly/2025/04/25/the-jobs-that-will-fall-first-as-ai-takes-over-the-workplace/.

[16] Ibid.

[17] Ibid.

[18] Ibid.

[19] Ibid.

[20] Ibid.

[21] Ibid.

[22] Ibid.

Lawrence, Kansas, doing little damage without injuries.[23] The vehicle, parked with the cab and trailer brakes engaged, began moving rapidly.[24] Regardless of the driver's efforts to keep pace, the truck drove through a four-foot retaining wall, crossed a patio, and traveled between two houses before slamming with a home's foundation.[25] The house directly struck suffered little damage, while the next residence was unharmed.[26] The semi-truck collided with powerlines, resulting in a fire beneath the truck.[27] This brings to the next point that I might not have mentioned in the previous book is how can Robo-Trucker determine if its brakes are in good shape. A hypothetical steep grade scenario was provided in the last book.

According to Adler (2023), the Federal Motor Carrier Safety Administration (FMCSA) has conducted an investigation into a highly publicized TuSimple autonomous truck crash.[28] TuSimple stated that it replied to many FMCSA requests following the non-injury event on Interstate 10 in Arizona.[29] The investigation concluded with no penalties.[30] The National Highway Traffic Safety Administration (NHTSA) declined to launch a separate investigation.[31] A driver-supervised autonomous truck made an unanticipated fast left turn across a westbound lane of traffic on I-10 and collided with a concrete barricade.[32] The safety driver attempted to countersteer the truck, which was following a computer-generated directive from many minutes before.[33] TuSimple first stated that the incident was due to driver mistake.[34] Later, it acknowledged that both its computing system and the safety driver bore culpability.[35]

The collision had a negative impact on TuSimple's top position among autonomous trucking firms.[36] It was the first to undertake a "driver out" pilot, known as Ghost Rider.[37] In December 2021, the truck with no human in the cab drove 80 miles at night from Tucson, Arizona, to a train yard east of Phoenix.[38] TuSimple did not immediately notify Navistar, its manufacturing partner at the time, of the disaster.[39] Navistar and TuSimple completed their 2-and-a-half-year relationship in late 2022, with the goal of developing a TuSimple-enabled International LT Class 8 truck for sale in 2025.[40]

---

[23] Sloan, Nick. "Driverless Semi-Truck Rolls through Lawrence Residential Area, Comes to Rest between Two Homes." KMBC, July 25, 2024. https://www.kmbc.com/article/driverless-semi-truck-rolls-through-lawrence-kansas-residential/61703544.

[24] Ibid.
[25] Ibid.
[26] Ibid.
[27] Ibid.
[28] Adler, Alan. "Feds Close Probe into Tusimple Autonomous Truck Crash." FreightWaves, March 2, 2023. https://www.freightwaves.com/news/feds-close-probe-into-tusimple-autonomous-truck-crash.

[29] Ibid.
[30] Ibid.
[31] Ibid.
[32] Ibid.
[33] Ibid.
[34] Ibid.
[35] Ibid.
[36] Ibid.
[37] Ibid.
[38] Ibid.
[39] Ibid.
[40] Ibid.

Which would bring to the Swiss Cheese Model of Safety Incident Causation and it could be used with any accident. According to Geraghty (2023), James Reason developed the Swiss Cheese Model of Incident Causation in 2000 for a British Medical Journal (BMJ) paper titled "Human error: models and management".[41] It is often utilized in risk assessment and management to explain how different degrees of protection might hypothetically stop failure.[42] In the model, Reason employs Swiss cheese slices to depict levels of protection against what he refers to as active failures and dormant circumstances.[43] Each level has "holes," or deficiencies, with the expectation that the flaws in all levels will not straighten and permit a hazard to cross through.[44] According to Reason's thesis, accidents are usually produced by four layers of failure: organizational effects, unsafe supervision, preconditions for dangerous behaviors, and unsafe acts themselves.[45]

To summarize, the problems depicted in the Swiss Cheese Model of Incident Causation would apply to Robo-Trucker including lack of human touch in control of the truck, no supervision if completely driverless, determinants for flaws, and the damages and violations themselves. No matter how anyone thinks that AI trucking is safe, but Robo-Trucker is still a danger to itself and to others.

Adeoye, et al. (2025) contend that AI is altering distribution and logistics by boosting efficiency, cutting expenses, and enhancing the delivery experience.[46] Some of the most important AI applications in this field is dynamic route optimization, in which machine learning (ML) algorithms examine instantaneous information such as traffic patterns, weather conditions, and road closures to consistently modify delivery routes.[47] This reduces gasoline use, improves delivery times, and avoids operational delays.[48] Autonomous delivery technologies, such as drones and self-driving trucks, are simultaneously changing last-mile and long-haul transportation by eliminating human interference while enhancing speed and dependability.[49] AI-powered automated delivery systems use modern technology like computer vision, ML, and sensors to determine real-time judgments.[50] Drones are used for time-sensitive deliveries in distant places, while autonomous trucks have the potential to transform long-distance freight transportation by offering round the clock performance, saving on expenses, and intensified safety measures.[51] Notwithstanding the obvious

---

[41] Geraghty, Tom. "The Swiss Cheese Model." Psych Safety, September 14, 2023. https://psychsafety.com/the-swiss-cheese-model/.

[42] Ibid.

[43] Ibid.

[44] Ibid.

[45] Ibid.

[46] Adeoye, Yetunde, Erumusele Francis Onotole, Tunde Ogunyankinnu, Godwin Aipoh, Akintunde Akinyele Osunkanmibi, and Joseph Egbemhenghe. "Artificial Intelligence in Logistics and Distribution: The Function of AI in Dynamic Route Planning for Transportation, Including Self-Driving Trucks and Drone Delivery Systems." *World Journal of Advanced Research and Reviews* 25, no. 2 (January 22, 2025): p. 155. https://doi.org/10.30574/wjarr.2025.25.2.0214.

[47] Ibid.

[48] Ibid.

[49] Ibid.

[50] Ibid.

[51] Ibid.

advantages, legal structures, security issues, and popular support still pose considerable impediments to widespread use.[52]

Route optimization aims to reduce transportation costs, time, and resources.[53] It is a crucial component of modern transportation logistics, in which companies try to bring items to clients as promptly while reducing gasoline consumption and operational costs.[54] Route optimization comprises selecting the optimum routes depending on various criteria, such as delivery timings, traffic patterns, road conditions, and vehicle capacity.[55] Previously, route preparation was done by hand with a map or atlas or with basic software that used fixed information.[56] Nevertheless, this technique has some disadvantages, including unanticipated traffic jams, changeable weather conditions, road closures, accidents, and fluctuating gasoline prices.[57] AI's capability to deal with enormous quantities of real-time information has revolutionized dynamic route optimization.[58] AI systems improve flexibility and efficiency by continuously adjusting routes depending on current information, unlike traditional systems that use static data.[59] AI-driven dynamic route optimization adjusts delivery routes based on real-time data from many sources, including accident databases, GPS devices, traffic sensors, and weather reports.[60] This enables logistics organizations to react swiftly to unanticipated occurrences such as inclement weather, road closures, or traffic congestion, which would otherwise delay planned deliveries.[61] For instance, if an accident or a traffic jam occurs on a scheduled route, the system can quickly recommend an alternate route to reduce delays and improve efficiency.[62] ML methods are particularly helpful in dynamic route optimization since they use past information to forecast future situations.[63] Algorithms can accurately anticipate routes by identifying traffic patterns, road usage, and weather conditions.[64]

This brings to the fact that GPS navigation systems are directing human truckers who are not familiar with certain routes to illegal roads which would result in striking low clearances and have major rollovers on sharp curves. In Newark, Delaware, DelTOT installed extra signage after truckers continuously striked a low clearance on Casho Mill Road as a result of paying attention to GPS (Payne, 2024).[65] The signage clearly indicated if the trucker did not use the turnaround when lights flashed that it would go kaboom.[66]

---

[52] Ibid.
[53] Ibid., p. 156
[54] Ibid.
[55] Ibid.
[56] Ibid.
[57] Ibid.
[58] Ibid.
[59] Ibid.
[60] Ibid.
[61] Ibid.
[62] Ibid.
[63] Ibid.
[64] Ibid.
[65] Payne, Greg. "Drivers Continue to Struggle with Warning System for Low Bridge." FOX 29 Philadelphia, August 29, 2024. https://www.fox29.com/news/drivers-continue-struggle-warning-system-low-bridge.

[66] Ibid.

In 1969, John Loudermilk released a ballad entitled "Interstate 40." The ballad lyrics included, "walkin' down the shoulder of Interstate 40, just a-cussin' every rock that I kick," and, "yeah, that's my life out on Interstate 40, but I'm a happy son of a gun. The government's given me Interstate 40 and the good Lord's give me a thumb." Interstate 40 is one of the longest interstate highways in the country. In Tennessee alone, it has had a share of issues from frequent construction zones to truck rollovers to sudden sinkholes. There are new attractions that are being built that would attract drivers off the road and would create traffic headaches. For example, a Buc-cees convenience store opened off of I-40 in 2023 to lure motorists heading towards Sevierville, Pigeon Forge, and Gatlinburg. Since then, it has resulted in traffic headaches although it is not considered a truck stop. According to Simpson (2023), the store opening resulted in a proposal of adding an extra interchange along I-40 to alleviate traffic congestion.[67]

According to WBBJ 7 Eyewitness News (2025), a FedEx truck ran off the road near Stanton, Tennessee, and struck trees, resulting in a fire.[68] This resulted in people losing their orders or gifts sent by loved ones. This goes to show that Robo-Trucker is liable to do the same thing and will destroy your packages regardless of value. It is also doubtful that it would recognize sinkholes.

There are more examples of human truck accidents on both interstate highways and two-lane roads that would be highly doubtful that Robo-Trucker would have common sense overcome. According to Jackson (2025), two dump trucks collided with each other on a highway near Shelbyville, Tennessee, resulting in the deaths of both human drivers.[69] According to Sneed (2015), 12 people perished and 42 more injured as a consequence of heavy fog along Interstate 75 near Calhoun, Tennessee, in 1990.[70] This resulted in one of the worst traffic accidents in Tennessee history.[71] The concern is can Robo-Trucker see through thick fog? According to Salvemini (2024), a semi-truck jackknifed another semi-truck near each other on I-40 East, while descending a 4% grade near Rockwood, Tennessee.[72] The accident was the result of freezing rain in the forecast.[73] According to Walton (2023), a tractor-trailer hauling corn collided into a car and a house after descending a 7% grade on U.S. Hwy. 41 in Jasper, Tennessee, resulting in a fatality.[74] The cause was failed

[67] Simpson, Carissa. "Largest Buc-Ee's in Country Opens in Sevierville." WVLT News, June 26, 2023. https://www.wvlt.tv/2023/06/26/largest-buc-ees-country-opens-sevierville/.

[68] WBBJ 7 Eyewitness News. "FedEx Truck Catches Fire after Crashing on I-40." WBBJ TV, March 25, 2025. https://www.wbbjtv.com/2025/03/25/fedex-truck-catches-fire-after-crashing-on-i-40/.

[69] Jackson, Aubriella. "2 Dump Truck Drivers Dead after Head-on Crash in Bedford County." WKRN News, March 11, 2025. https://www.wkrn.com/news/local-news/2-dump-truck-drivers-dead-after-head-on-crash-in-bedford-county/.

[70] Sneed, Calvin. "'Stumbling out of the Fog:' Memories of the Worst Traffic Accident in Tennessee History." WTVC, December 11, 2015. https://newschannel9.com/news/local/stumbling-out-of-the-fog-memories-of-the-worst-traffic-accident-in-tennessee-history.

[71] Ibid.
[72] Salvemini, Chris. "TDOT: Jackknifed Semi-Truck Blocks I-40 East near Rockwood in Roane County | Wbir.Com." WBIR News, January 19, 2024. https://www.wbir.com/article/traffic/roane-county-crash-i-40-east-january-18-2024/51-e36b172a-1aef-405e-a98b-81e640d8674b.

[73] Ibid.
[74] Walton, Abbey. "Photos: 1 Dead after Tractor-Trailer Strikes Jasper Home Wednesday." WTVC, July 27, 2023.

brakes and speeding off of the Cumberland Plateau.[75] Robo-trucker would not be able to smell or see smoke when brakes are failing going down a steep grade regardless of where it happens. I mentioned in the previous book that dangerous terrain such as Wolf Creek Pass in Colorado and the "Monteagle Meltdown" in Tennessee are untrusted places for AI trucking.

According to Maher (2022), autonomous trucks will provide significant savings to transportation corporations, as driver expenses contribute for around 40% of trucking costs.[76] This could be tough to persuade a skeptical group of citizens to share the road with large autonomous trucks, but if the industry can handle the challenge and the project is not terminated after the first fatality, everyone should win—except, of course, truckers who would perish.[77] There are many truckers; over two million workers earn good income moving freight on America's highways.[78] They will not disappear suddenly, and several individuals will still be working in the industry.[79] However, autonomous long-distance trucks pose a danger to many decent positions, which are currently held mostly by American men with no postsecondary education.[80] The trucking business will migrate away from relatively high-paying employment and toward lower-paying ones.[81] Long-haul truckers who do little more than drive will be the first to be laid off, as their labor is easily automated, unlike drivers who load and unload freight.[82] Over the road (OTR) truckers typically older, higher-paid, and most likely to be affiliated with a union, such as the Teamsters, versus short-haul truckers.[83] Delivery drivers, usually freelancers, have difficulties paying expenses, would not be replaced by machines in the near future.[84] This trend will tend to degrade living conditions for those with low socioeconomic status, making inequality and associated social issues worse.[85] Throughout the 40 years following the Second World War, technological advances created "productivity effects" which boosted overall standards of living.[86] Since 1987, however, technological advances have eliminated more employment than they were generated, making people develop lower socioeconomic status, with no equivalent gains in productivity.[87] The task for policymakers is serious and urgent.[88] When more people without college degrees lose income and are cannot pay their bills, it will lead to despair-related mortality such as heart disease, substance abuse, and

https://newschannel9.com/news/local/1-dead-after-tractor-trailer-strikes-jasper-home-wednesday-night-marion-county-tennessee.

[75] Ibid.

[76] Maher, Stephen. "What Happens When Human Truckers Are Replaced by AI?" Newsweek, February 3, 2022. https://www.newsweek.com/what-happens-when-human-truckers-are-replaced-ai-opinion-1675106.

[77] Ibid.
[78] Ibid.
[79] Ibid.
[80] Ibid.
[81] Ibid.
[82] Ibid.
[83] Ibid.
[84] Ibid.
[85] Ibid.
[86] Ibid.
[87] Ibid.
[88] Ibid.

suicide.[89] This tendency has a connection with a rise of backing for populist authoritarian governments.[90]

AI continues to assist disabled individuals in becoming more independent and that would be the only form of AI that could be trusted. Mangrolia, Panchal, and Patel (2024) suggest that technology can help individuals with disabilities achieve independence, increase quality of life, and enhance social interactions.[91] People with mobility difficulties can get around more readily thanks to assistive devices including wheelchairs, motorized scooters, and exoskeletons.[92] Hearing aids can help those with hearing loss hear sounds more clearly.[93] To enhance communication, technology options include sign language translation and augmentative and alternative communication (AAC).[94] People with disabilities benefit from a range of technical tools, such as screen readers, magnifiers, voice recognition, accessible software, smart home technologies, and job and educational supports.[95] Many technological devices require manual operation, making it difficult for individuals with disabilities to operate them independently.[96] The disabled individual has only become autonomous through the employment of AI-powered devices.[97]

A prosthesis replaces or enhances a missing or dysfunctional physical component, either externally or through implantation.[98] BCI (Brain-Computer Interface) systems with AI capabilities can be utilized to design prosthetics.[99] BCIs enable humans to interact with automated devices, like prosthetic or robotic limbs, utilizing their brain activity rather than their muscles.[100] A BCI converts user-generated brain activity patterns into commands using AI-powered Smart Prosthetic Hands.[101] The peripheral nerve interface is a more effective option for controlling prosthetic limbs than electromyography (EMG).[102] This method uses implanted electrodes to read impulses directly from nerves, rather than skin sensors.[103] Assistive robotics aims to empower those with limited mobility to complete activities autonomously.[104] AI algorithms improve human-machine interactions, leading to more efficient and intuitive systems.[105] AI-powered smart wheelchairs can navigate, respond to voice commands, and avoid obstructions.[106]

---

[89] Ibid.

[90] Ibid.

[91] Mangrolia, Jayandrath R., Disha D Panchal, and Keyur Patel. "The Role of Artificial Intelligence in Overcoming Disabilities: Challenges, Innovations, and Future Directions." *Cuestiones de Fisioterapia* 53, no. 1 (2024): p. 241.

[92] Ibid.

[93] Ibid.

[94] Ibid.

[95] Ibid.

[96] Ibid.

[97] Ibid.

[98] Ibid.

[99] Ibid., p. 241-242

[100] Ibid., p. 242

[101] Ibid.

[102] Ibid.

[103] Ibid.

[104] Ibid.

[105] Ibid.

[106] Ibid.

People who are visually impaired can tremendously benefit from AI techniques.[107] Computer vision-based assistive technology is a rapidly growing sector for the visually impaired.[108] Assistive technology can help visually impaired individuals gain independence.[109] Assisting individuals with daily chores such as finding doors, losing items, moving indoors and outdoors, and identifying impediments.[110] Although there are numerous assistive technologies available for the blind, their complicated designs make them expensive to build on a commercial basis.[111] Wearable technology, such as smart glasses, employs AI to describe environments for those with vision problems.[112]

AI systems analyze massive volumes of educational data to identify trends and predict outcomes.[113] AI can evaluate student behaviors, performance indicators, and engagement levels in the context of learning impairments in order to detect early warning signs of learning disorders.[114] This enables instructors to develop tailored learning plans and implement targeted interventions that address each student's distinct requirements.[115] AI's ability to continuously assess and alter learning courses ensures that youngsters receive the assistance they need to thrive.[116] Individualized Learning and AI Tutoring Systems support persons with learning difficulties through individualized education platforms.[117] Various adaptive learning solutions based on AI have been created that modify content complexity, instructional techniques, and pace to individual needs.[118] In case of cognitive disabilities, AI systems can help those with cognitive disorders, such as autism, Down's syndrome, or dementia, by offering reminders, scheduling, and communication support.[119] There are highlight technologies that improve memory or provide structured routines.[120] AI can assist individuals with autism spectrum disorders (ASD) build social skills by simulating interactions through applications and virtual agents.[121]

Disabled individuals seeking healthcare is an increasing global phenomenon, according to Arasi, et al. (2025).[122] Long-term care provides nursing, complex medical, recovery, and public entitlement programs such as Supplemental Nutrition Assistance Program (SNAP), Medicaid, and Supplemental Security Income

---

[107] Ibid., p. 243
[108] Ibid.
[109] Ibid.
[110] Ibid.
[111] Ibid.
[112] Ibid.
[113] Ibid., p. 245
[114] Ibid.
[115] Ibid.
[116] Ibid.
[117] Ibid.
[118] Ibid.
[119] Ibid.
[120] Ibid.
[121] Ibid.
[122] Arasi, Munya A., Hussah Nasser AlEisa, Amani A. Alneil, and Radwa Marzouk. "Artificial Intelligence-Driven Ensemble Deep Learning Models for Smart Monitoring of Indoor Activities in IOT Environment for People with Disabilities." *Scientific Reports* 15, no. 1 (February 5, 2025): p. 1. https://doi.org/10.1038/s41598-025-88450-1.

(SSI).[123] It is very expensive, but sophisticated technologies can assist in spending reductions by certifying excellent health care and improving the quality of life.[124] The revolutionary potential of the Internet of Things (IoT) extends the lives of almost one billion people globally with impairments.[125] The IoT delivers sophisticated solutions to various activities that individuals with impairments face, while also promoting equality.[126] Behavioral identification techniques are technological fields which examine a description of an individual's conduct or motions based on information captured by pictures, smartphones, video frames, and sensors worn around the body.[127] They are effective in verifying functions such as action detection, key function observation, and tracking.[128] Traditional deep learning (DL) and ML algorithms are effective in detecting human behavior.[129]

More than one billion people globally, or roughly 15% of the population, identify as having multiple disabilities.[130] These disorders may appear in childhood or improve with age, such as reduced hand function from a stroke.[131] Individuals with disabilities face significant challenges in managing their household appliances daily.[132] Classical residences were renovated into smart homes to improve living conditions for disabled individuals.[133] Previously, IoT technology was designed to allow devices to communicate without human intervention.[134] Nowadays, IoT technology is integrated into home devices, allowing them to operate the internet remotely.[135] IoT is defined as the use of software, sensors, and technologies to connect physical objects to other devices over the internet.[136] Light switches that respond to thermostats or power commands can save energy use by adjusting the indoor temperatures.[137] Authors offer several ways for enabling impaired individuals to control devices remotely via IoT using voice commands or smartphone GUIs.[138] Human Activity Recognition (HAR) is the science of identifying actions or movements using smartphone or wearable sensor information in images or video frames.[139]

These behaviors are implemented indoors, such as sitting, standing, walking, and taking the stairs.[140] It is also critical to determine the locations where practical tasks are carried out.[141] Computer technologies and

---

[123] Ibid.
[124] Ibid.
[125] Ibid.
[126] Ibid.
[127] Ibid.
[128] Ibid.
[129] Ibid.
[130] Ibid.
[131] Ibid.
[132] Ibid.
[133] Ibid.
[134] Ibid.
[135] Ibid.
[136] Ibid., p. 2
[137] Ibid.
[138] Ibid.
[139] Ibid.
[140] Ibid.
[141] Ibid.

movements by humans were used to better perceive artificial vision.[142] HAR has various applications, including security against terrorism, help, lifelogging, and surveillance.[143] These strategies were proven to be useful for providing appropriate home care for the disabled, as well as indoor tracking systems.[144] With a growing number of disabled and elderly individuals, there is a greater need for assistance for individuals who have lost mobility and wish to remain in their homes, necessitating ongoing community care.[145] Indoor communication channels are less likely to deviate from their environment than outdoor ones.[146] It depends on a number of elements, including building structure, construction materials, and room arrangement.[147] The Indoor Positioning System (IPS) uses a network of receivers and transmitters to offer real-time location of individuals or things in various situations.[148] HAR is described as the talent of utilizing AI to recognize and name activities acquired from raw data using many resources.[149] Advancements in ML and DL have resulted in usable methods for extracting features using unprocessed data from sensors[150] The growing worldwide predominance of impairments emphasizes the need for appropriate remedies that enhance the quality of life for those afflicted.[151] Individuals with cognitive or physical limitations typically struggle to manage daily duties, including controlling their living environment.[152] As linked devices and smart technologies progress, there is an increasing possibility of creating systems that empower and support persons with disabilities.[153] Intelligent monitoring systems improve household management, promoting independence and safety.[154] Integrating enhanced DL approaches into an IoT ecosystem can transform smart home design, offering customized solutions for various demands.[155]

Binkley, Reynolds, and Shuman (2025) argue that while other organizations have noted the issue of prejudice in AI, there has been little focus on the possible harms and benefits that AI models may offer to disabled individuals.[156] AI models may discriminate against disabled patients in three ways: underrepresentation in datasets, discrimination in medical care, and overestimation of physiological frailty.[157] The disability community is smaller than the general population, and most healthcare data used to train AI models comes from healthy patients.[158] While AI models trained on non-disabled patients can reliably predict outcomes, they fall short when applied to impaired individuals.[159] Additionally, health data

---

[142] Ibid.
[143] Ibid.
[144] Ibid.
[145] Ibid.
[146] Ibid.
[147] Ibid.
[148] Ibid.
[149] Ibid.
[150] Ibid.
[151] Ibid.
[152] Ibid.
[153] Ibid.
[154] Ibid.
[155] Ibid.
[156] Ibid., p. 12
[157] Ibid.
[158] Ibid.
[159] Ibid.

for impaired people may be absent or incomplete.[160] Data underrepresentation and misrepresentation can lead to bias and discrimination.[161]

Historical data may reflect healthcare practitioners' biases toward disabled patients, which are based on doctors' assessments of a disabled patient's quality of life, worthiness, and perceived futility of treatment.[162] Disabled people are frequently denied required and, in some cases, life-saving treatments because of their disability, rather than an objective assessment of medical indication and treatment efficacy.[163] AI models based on historical data may indicate that impaired individuals have higher disease-specific and overall mortality rates.[164] However, impaired individuals die more frequently, not only because the health consequences of a disability are strongly connected to higher morbidity and mortality, but also because they are simply not given the appropriate therapies.[165]

According to Davidson (2025), disabled persons have higher discrimination risks when working with AI and algorithmic systems.[166] Initially, many AI and algorithmic devices are taught to recognize patterns and make choices according to prevalent trends within a particular dataset.[167] Nevertheless, many disabled individuals exist outside of traditional patterns due to their impairment, such as gait variances, speech differences, unique eye movements, and so on.[168] Certain tools may unintentionally discriminate against people with certain types of disability, especially if they depend on biometric inputs.[169] Secondly, AI and algorithmic technologies generate outputs depending on inputs obtained from datasets (also known as "training data").[170] These datasets frequently fail to include disabled individuals– they may contain incorrect disability data, undersample, or incorrectly tag information as disability-related.[171] All of this can result in AI systems that discriminate against disabled people, thereby worsening their plight.[172] Thirdly, several disabled individuals are multi-marginalized, which means they are impaired and also identify with another marginalized group.[173] Several AI and algorithmic devices have been discovered to provide particular dangers to other disadvantaged populations, meaning that individuals with multiple disabilities are more vulnerable to discriminatory outcomes as a consequence of how they interact with the tools.[174]

---

[160] Ibid.

[161] Ibid.

[162] Ibid.

[163] Ibid.

[164] Ibid.

[165] Ibid.

[166] Davidson, Jess. "Report: Building a Disability-Inclusive AI Ecosystem: A Cross-Disability, Cross-Systems Analysis of Best Practices." AAPD, March 11, 2025. https://www.aapd.com/disability-inclusive-ai/.

[167] Ibid.

[168] Ibid.

[169] Ibid.

[170] Ibid.

[171] Ibid.

[172] Ibid.

[173] Ibid.

[174] Ibid.

According to Lay-Flurrie (2025), mobility is an essential entitlement for disabled individuals, and it streamlines technological advances for everyone.[175] Copilot for Microsoft 365 is boosting efficiency at work never previously; over ten million individuals employ Microsoft Edge monthly to have the internet read out loud; more than 1 million people use Immersive Reader to make websites simpler to read; and collaborators such as Tobii Dynavox and Special Olympics are providing AI to disabled individuals around the world.[176]

According to Hossian (2024), AI may additionally empower disabled individuals by providing customized assistance and resources that can be used based on their requirements and preferences, such as summarizing phone conversations, documents, or emails, performing 'plain language' writing transformation, and helping with drafting through recommended text.[177] Yet in the job field, AI-driven intelligence or personality assessments utilized during the selection process may disfavor impaired candidates when compared to able-bodied candidates.[178] For example, if test platforms are inaccessible to visually handicapped candidates using screen readers.[179]

According to Pochechuev (2025), AI-powered sign language interpreters can translate movements into words that are spoken or written.[180] It implies that live translation from sign to verbal languages can help persons with disabilities communicate more effectively and make whole between them and the remainder of society.[181] Furthermore, it is worthwhile to mention AI-powered hearing devices with noise reduction.[182] They may enhance readability by blocking out noises from the background, making it easier to hear in crowded environments.[183]

I recently visited the dentist and noticed that they are using an AI dental X-ray system, which looked very confusing. It is to detect where a patient had treatment, any additional damage, and additional treatment to be planned in the future. It is basically to speed up the timing of diagnostics.

---

[175] Lay-Flurrie, Jenny. "Microsoft Ability Summit 2025: Accessibility in the AI Era." The Official Microsoft Blog, March 18, 2025. https://blogs.microsoft.com/blog/2025/03/18/microsoft-ability-summit-2025-accessibility-in-the-ai-era/.

[176] Ibid.

[177] Hossian, Fadeia. "Inclusive AI for People with Disabilities: Key Considerations." Clifford Chance, December 3, 2024. https://www.cliffordchance.com/insights/resources/blogs/talking-tech/en/articles/2024/12/inclusive-ai-for-people-with-disabilities--key-considerations.html.

[178] Ibid.
[179] Ibid.
[180] Pochechuev, Artem. "AI for Disabilities: Quick Overview, Challenges, and the Road Ahead." SwissCognitive, January 7, 2025. https://swisscognitive.ch/2025/01/07/ai-for-disabilities-quick-overview-challenges-and-the-road-ahead/.

[181] Ibid.
[182] Ibid.
[183] Ibid.

2 AI IN RETAIL

According to Spencer (2024), AI in retail is revitalizing the industry by supporting retailers in improving their business processes, developing new methods to engage with customers, and upgrading the customer experience (CX).[184] Personalization is the next frontier for retail business, but the world's digitally aware buyers have continuously shifted tastes and expect bespoke, quick, and seamless purchasing experiences.[185] AI is the ultimate instrument for meeting these expectations, thanks to its capacity to instinctively comprehend user desires and create individualized services.[186] But remaining successful entails more than just providing experiences that foster loyalty.[187] Retailers face numerous problems, including geopolitical turmoil, economic unpredictability, and the climate issue.[188] While traditional techniques may be losing traction, AI provides a strategic perspective, providing cutting-edge analytics and forecasts to help merchants respond quickly to market changes.[189]

According to Marotta (2024), the retail industry's digital transition has been ongoing for several years.[190] It has enhanced speed, efficiency, and accuracy across all sectors of the retail industry, thanks in significant part to sophisticated information and predictive analytics tools that help firms make

---

[184] Spencer, Amanda. "Artificial Intelligence in Retail: 6 Use Cases and Examples." Forbes, April 19, 2024. https://www.forbes.com/sites/sap/2024/04/19/artificial-intelligence-in-retail-6-use-cases-and-examples/.

[185] Ibid.

[186] Ibid.

[187] Ibid.

[188] Ibid.

[189] Ibid.

[190] Marotta, Deb. "Artificial Intelligence: How AI Is Changing Retail." Hitachi Solutions, April 2, 2024. https://global.hitachi-solutions.com/blog/ai-in-retail/.

data-driven decisions.[191] None of these insights would be conceivable without the IoT and, more significantly, AI.[192] AI in retail has supplied companies access to high-level information and data, which is utilized to improve customer service and provide new business opportunities.[193] In fact, AI in retail is expected to have generated $40 billion in additional sales over the course of three years.[194]

Buehler (2024) states that Tractor Supply Company has incorporated AI in its logistics, personnel, and marketing and sales operations.[195] Its primary focus is client service; hence AI has helped Tractor Supply improve their service.[196] It employs an AI-powered tech assistant named "Gura," which means "great, uncover, recover, and ask."[197] Any store employee may utilize this device to provide excellent customer service.[198] Consider the following scenario: a customer is searching for a dog food that is appropriate for sensitive skin.[199] A store employee may utilize Gura to assess which commodities are most suitable for the consumer, and it can also discover the amount of inventory and prices of a certain sort of food in the present moment.[200]

Among the primary benefits of adding AI into store leadership is the potential to provide customized experiences while shopping.[201] AI algorithms use large quantities of precious client information, such as browsing habits, preferences, and purchase history, to generate personalized suggestions.[202] Amazon excels in using AI technologies to generate personalized consumer suggestions.[203] Its AI program employs ML to recommend items according to a consumer's purchase history and the habits of related customers.[204] The application not just improves client happiness, but it additionally boosts revenue by presenting customers with pertinent products according to statistical data.[205] Amazon's unique "high return rate" message additionally redirects users' queries to the customer review section of an item's page, allowing consumers to decide whether an item is worth

---

[191] Ibid.

[192] Ibid.

[193] Ibid.

[194] Ibid.

[195] Buehler, T Leigh. "Artificial Intelligence in Retail and Improving Efficiency: American Public University." APU, March 4, 2025. https://www.apu.apus.edu/area-of-study/business-and-management/resources/artificial-intelligence-in-retail-and-improving-efficiency/.

[196] Ibid.

[197] Ibid.

[198] Ibid.

[199] Ibid.

[200] Ibid.

[201] Ibid.

[202] Ibid.

[203] Ibid.

[204] Ibid.

[205] Ibid.

purchasing or returning.[206] This AI-powered approach also aids in the management of Amazon's reverse logistics and inventory systems.[207]

Businesses can improve their inventory management systems by incorporating AI into demand forecasts.[208] AI examines past sales figures, external factors, and market trends.[209] Subsequently, it anticipates prospective consumer appetite for goods more precisely than traditional forecasting methods.[210] A notable data analysis example is Walmart's utilization of AI to forecast which items would be requested during various seasons.[211] This excellent analysis allows for better inventory management and decreases the likelihood of overstock or shortages of goods.[212] AI improves Walmart's daily logistical processes and predicts demand phases, particularly when there are peak periods or unexpected increases in consumer traffic.[213] However, it is vital to stress that Walmart mandated a multiyear approach to collect relevant information and create the application as needed to design modifiable algorithms for its AI application.[214] Utilizing AI required a significant expenditure of money, time, and personnel, yet it turned back for Walmart by providing customers with an additional streamlined buying experience.[215]

AI technologies may streamline various operational operations within a business, which is especially beneficial to major merchants.[216] The goal is to improve resource usage, lower costs, eliminate errors, and boost production.[217] AI in the management of supply chains enables continuous monitoring and capacity for forecasting.[218] Shopping organizations may employ AI to monitor deliveries, check the stock quantities, and recognize possible problems with the supply chain.[219] As a consequence, productivity increases and expenses decrease.[220] H&M, a Swedish fashion retailer, employs AI to manage logistics, monitor patterns, and estimate consumer demand, allowing it to respond quickly to evolving market demands and cut lead times.[221] The retailer's AI technology is

---

[206] Ibid.
[207] Ibid.
[208] Ibid.
[209] Ibid.
[210] Ibid.
[211] Ibid.
[212] Ibid.
[213] Ibid.
[214] Ibid.
[215] Ibid.
[216] Ibid.
[217] Ibid.
[218] Ibid.
[219] Ibid.
[220] Ibid.
[221] Ibid.

ideal for rapid fashion; the application collects information from blogs and search engines, allowing AI algorithms to analyze and forecast trends.[222] The information assists H&M executives make purchasing decisions, such as what amount to spend, how to purchase it, and how to put it in shops.[223] The AI data also assists H&M predict when to refill a popular item and how many buyers are likely to be interested in that item.[224] H&M can cut waste while making environmentally friendly choices by optimizing its supply chain with AI.[225]

According to Downie and Hayes (2024), AI-powered virtual assistants and chatbots offer immediate assistance to clients by answering questions, expediting the purchase process, and resolving concerns.[226] These techniques are becoming more complex with natural language processing (NLP), allowing for human-like discussions.[227] Retailers may utilize chatbots on websites or applications to assist customers in navigating product offerings, checking order progress, or troubleshooting issues.[228] Virtual shopping companions help clients navigate the online experience by making product recommendations and nurturing leads through a sales funnel.[229] With the expanding capacity of generative AI, chatbots and virtual assistants may now automate complex client experiences.[230] Customers may now use AI-assisted search and augmented reality to find and research products before making a purchase.[231] For example, AI can evaluate photographs provided by users and recommend visually comparable products.[232] This has gained popularity in fashion and home design, where customers may be looking for visually comparable products.[233] Similarly, AI-enhanced AR enables shoppers to "try on" things before purchasing.[234] Fashion and beauty firms such as Sephora have had early success with tools that allow shoppers to preview how apparel or makeup would look before committing to a product.[235]

Demand forecasting predicts future product demand using advanced data analytics and ML

---

[222] Ibid.

[223] Ibid.

[224] Ibid.

[225] Ibid.

[226] Downie, Amanda, and Molly Hayes. "AI in Retail." IBM, October 10, 2024. https://www.ibm.com/think/topics/ai-in-retail.

[227] Ibid.

[228] Ibid.

[229] Ibid.

[230] Ibid.

[231] Ibid.

[232] Ibid.

[233] Ibid.

[234] Ibid.

[235] Ibid.

models.[236] These technologies enable firms to plan more efficiently by combining sales data, customer data, and third-party data such as market trends.[237] AI algorithms can scan huge amounts of information and discover tendencies that traditional methods may miss, making them more accurate than earlier forecasting systems.[238] Retailers may better manage inventories and optimize logistics by accurately predicting demand.[239] These models also assist firms in responding rapidly to unforeseen conditions or market developments by giving data-driven insights into future events.[240] Demand forecasting using ML has made an enormous effect on the grocery business.[241] As an instance, several firms use automated daily ordering in their fresh-food sections to boost product availability and prevent waste.[242]

AI can help a retail organization manage its backend operations, such as inventory and supply chain management.[243] Organizations may improve inventories, boost visibility, cut costs, and eliminate errors by incorporating AI technologies into various supply chain operations such as supplier management and transportation logistics.[244] In the retail industry, AI algorithms optimize transportation routes, shorten delivery times, and change schedules to meet specified requirements such as carbon emissions thresholds.[245] They are also used to automate certain portions of the inventory and supplier management processes, such as restocking low-stock items or minimizing the amount of manual labor necessary to place orders.[246] These tools can assist an organization speed up operations, maintain optimal inventory levels, and decrease human error.[247] Walmart, for example, employs AI to improve delivery vehicles, routing them through more efficient paths and studying weather trends to guarantee that goods arrive on time.[248]

AI is rapidly being utilized to safeguard shops and customers against loss prevention and fraud.[249] AI systems can examine transaction patterns and spot anomalies that may suggest fraudulent activity,

---

[236] Ibid.
[237] Ibid.
[238] Ibid.
[239] Ibid.
[240] Ibid.
[241] Ibid.
[242] Ibid.
[243] Ibid.
[244] Ibid.
[245] Ibid.
[246] Ibid.
[247] Ibid.
[248] Ibid.
[249] Ibid.

assisting retailers in avoiding losses.[250] AI solutions can also improve cybersecurity in online payments by monitoring online transactions and client accounts for potential data breaches, hence boosting the security of ecommerce platforms.[251] Many financial institutions and huge internet platforms, such as eBay, use automated fraud detection software to identify possible difficulties.[252] In recent years, some stores have adopted AI-assisted loss prevention systems.[253] These are used to evaluate in-store data and detect potential theft.[254]

According to Kuo (2025), today's retailers face an impossible situation.[255] Rampant shoplifting is devouring corporate margins.[256] Shoplifting incidences have increased 93% since the pre-Covid period.[257] The strategies used by companies to handle the problem are alienating customers and undermining total sales.[258] This dilemma impacts not just large chains such as Walgreens, but also small enterprises with much smaller profit margins.[259] Mom-and-pop business owners in New York City are living in fear of the next retail attack, forcing them to allow only one or two customers into their stores at a time.[260] Clearly, retail thievery is not sustainable.[261] It reduces revenues, demoralizes employees, and drives away customers.[262] Locking merchandise or having customers wait simply exacerbates the problem.[263] Retailers must find a method to secure inventory and personnel while retaining customers.[264] Notably, a new technology has emerged: enhanced video security.[265] Yes, retailers have utilized video surveillance for decades, but antiquated closed-circuit television (CCTV) cannot compete with modern technologies.[266] Modern video security provides cloud-based flexibility and proactive deterrence, offering merchants a realistic chance to strike back.[267]

The ordinary chain pharmacy store may appear easy to the consumer, but retailers understand

---

[250] Ibid.
[251] Ibid.
[252] Ibid.
[253] Ibid.
[254] Ibid.
[255] Ibid.
[256] Ibid.
[257] Ibid.
[258] Ibid.
[259] Ibid.
[260] Ibid.
[261] Ibid.
[262] Ibid.
[263] Ibid.
[264] Ibid.
[265] Ibid.
[266] Ibid.
[267] Ibid.

how intricate these places are.[268] On any one day, hundreds, if not thousands, of consumers may enter and exit.[269] Merchandise is constantly lifted and set aside, as personnel rush around trying to accommodate the needs of eager consumers.[270] Managers and security personnel can undoubtedly monitor some of this activity, but their perspective will always be limited, even with the help of traditional CCTV.[271] Raw video of fast-moving client scenarios may only tell so much—and even the largest chains lack the resources to constantly filter through and evaluate all of that data.[272] This new form of video security provides retailers with unparalleled, complete intelligence.[273] They can take raw video and immediately identify troubling behavior thanks to ML algorithms trained on vast retail-specific datasets.[274] They, like all-seeing security guards, see the telltale indicators of an impending crime.[275] The deterrent advantages are enormous.[276] This technology can help on-site security staff by providing real-time monitoring and notifications.[277] Stopping a shoplifter in the process of stealing can be dangerous, and many store regulations discourage it, especially if the item's value is less than the felony threshold.[278] Of course, it is precisely these little, uncorrected thefts that contribute to fatal profit reduction.[279] However, if a security guard is able to track down a specific individual of interest using AI, their sheer presence can prevent the heist from occurring.[280] Some may be concerned about privacy and the usage of AI technology in video security.[281] However, there is technology available that tracks people and objects using an algorithm known as "similarity search," rather than facial recognition.[282] This system can analyze footage in real time or during playback to accurately locate where a target has appeared.[283] This system does not employ face recognition data or require individuals to register in advance, and no personally identifiable information (PII) is collected or processed.[284] Instead, the object is issued a random number, which is then compared to other video objects to find a match.[285] Furthermore, advanced video surveillance can help merchants

[268] Ibid.
[269] Ibid.
[270] Ibid.
[271] Ibid.
[272] Ibid.
[273] Ibid.
[274] Ibid.
[275] Ibid.
[276] Ibid.
[277] Ibid.
[278] Ibid.
[279] Ibid.
[280] Ibid.
[281] Ibid.
[282] Ibid.
[283] Ibid.
[284] Ibid.
[285] Ibid.

construct a case against repeat offenders and even reclaim damages.[286] This device can register each stolen item over numerous trips without endangering security personnel, until the overall value surpasses the felony level, at which point law police can be contacted.[287] This quiet, discreet method pays deterrent dividends even beyond the individual case, as would-be felony shoplifters learn that the store uses this technology and decide not to take the risk in the first place.[288]

The advancements are strongly related to the advent of Video Surveillance as a Service (VSaaS), a shockingly underappreciated aspect of the entire SaaS revolution.[289] VSaaS solutions are especially beneficial for chains that require high levels of coordination and centralization across dozens or hundreds of outlets.[290] VSasS offers complete security systems that can be accessed from anywhere, allowing them to send action alerts at the individual store level while also providing company headquarters with full, synthesized insights into their overall business operation.[291] One reason this is significant is the influence that layout and social engineering play in theft deterrent.[292] Stores are frequently busier at certain times than others; customers will naturally congregate in certain areas of the store while others remain relatively uncongested.[293] Retailers are constantly triaging, scrambling to consider all of these elements and discover the most efficient methods to organize merchandise and distribute workers.[294] Cloud-based VSaaS solutions can help streamline this process by removing uncertainty, highlighting bottlenecks and blind spots, and informing retailers about what actually works.[295] Unfortunately, in many circumstances, employees steal from their employers.[296] VSaaS systems, along with robust, integrated access restrictions, may additionally serve an essential part in this regard.[297] A degree of theft will always be unavoidable: it is simply the cost of doing business.[298] However, the increase in theft that shops had dealt with in recent years cannot continue: If these figures continue to climb, the consequences will be devastating.[299] The new VSaaS solutions have arisen as a bright light in an otherwise dark moment for retail, and they are already helping to

---

[286] Ibid.
[287] Ibid.
[288] Ibid.
[289] Ibid.
[290] Ibid.
[291] Ibid.
[292] Ibid.
[293] Ibid.
[294] Ibid.
[295] Ibid.
[296] Ibid.
[297] Ibid.
[298] Ibid.
[299] Ibid.

turn the tide of the crisis.[300] Their benefits are only just beginning to be recognized, particularly in terms of using real-time data to deter crime and enabling faster response times to avoid theft.[301]

According to Oosthuizen (2021), digital disruption occurs when new digital technologies impact the structure and operations of businesses, transforming internal business processes, changing customer interactions to drive experiences, and altering how value is created across business models.[302] New technologies challenge established business models by altering marketplaces, introducing new competition, and altering the client purchasing journey.[303] The digital era's rapid expansion is driven by advancements in computing power, mobile connectivity, data availability, and cost-effective technologies.[304] Recent advancements in computing power and lower storage costs have led to digital disruption across industries.[305] Examples of industrial transformations include the music business's transition from vinyl to digital, merchants' transition from brick-and-mortar stores to online platforms, the medical industry's use of robots for surgery, and news organizations' shift from physical to digital mediums.[306] Furthermore, the rate and pace at which new technologies enter and change the market has expanded tremendously, and the combinations of these technologies have unforeseeable repercussions where market boundaries are blurred.[307] Thus, the digital era is one of society's most fundamental developments, encompassing many aspects of business and daily life.[308] Digital disruption is driven by AI, blockchain, big data, augmented reality, IoT, 3D printing, and cloud computing technologies.[309] AI is at the forefront of disruptive technology.[310] AI now plays a large role in our daily activities, such as unlocking phones through facial recognition, tailoring material on social media, and navigating to work.[311] AI systems are transforming the business landscape by approving home loans, flagging inappropriate comments on news platforms, predicting patient outcomes in clinical trials, enabling human-robot interaction in factories, tracking items in warehouses, and managing customer relationships for wholesalers, among other applications. [312] Retailers are implementing new technology, such as AI-powered solutions, to stay competitive in

---

[300] Ibid.

[301] Ibid.

[302] Oosthuizen, Kim. "Artificial Intelligence in Retail: The AI-Enabled Value Chain," 2021, p. 1.

[303] Ibid.

[304] Ibid.

[305] Ibid.

[306] Ibid.

[307] Ibid.

[308] Ibid.

[309] Ibid.

[310] Ibid.

[311] Ibid.

[312] Ibid.

today's diverse customer market.[313] Major retailers who engaged in AI are seeing economic benefits.[314]

Anica-Popa, et al. (2021) argue that the increase of e-commerce and customer data has led organizations to seek ways to predict customer behavior and enhance the consumer experience (CE).[315] Appropriate ownership of data, evaluation, and exploitation can result in an edge in competition for businesses.[316] Linguistic recognition systems, also referred to as chatbots, improve CE by delivering services around the clock while dramatically reducing the number of poor-quality exchanges that require staff members.[317] These technologies are presently gaining prominence due to messaging applications.[318] Retailers utilize chatbots to integrate offline and online interactions.[319] For instance, in 2016, H&M outperformed its rivals by developing a chatbot that operated on the Canadian messaging service Kik, which allowed shoppers to discover, contribute, and purchase items from the H&M catalog.[320] The chatbot additionally provided a personal stylist experience by leveraging photo picks and asking inquiries regarding the purchaser's fashion, resulting in a fashion profile for the client.[321]

Voice recognition technologies employ virtual assistants to conduct duties such as processing phone orders, searching for information, and making personalized recommendations to customers.[322] The customer's voice command is converted to text and sent for order taking devices instantly or by email.[323] McDonald's Corporation has created a complicated, automated ordering mechanism that supports multiple languages and accents.[324] Visual recognition technologies enable virtual assistants to detect forms or individuals, follow the progress of product shipments, create accounts from home, and assess online consumer tastes for specific brands.[325] For instance, a merchant may utilize face recognition technology to recognize a regular consumer or loyalty

---

[313] Ibid., p. 2

[314] Ibid.

[315] Anica-Popa, Ionut, Liana Anica-Popa, Cristina Radulescu, and Marinela Vrincianu. "The Integration of Artificial Intelligence in Retail: Benefits, Challenges and a Dedicated Conceptual Framework." *Amfiteatru Economic Journal* 23, no. 56 (February 2021): p. 122. https://doi.org/10.24818/ea/2021/56/120.

[316] Ibid.

[317] Ibid.

[318] Ibid.

[319] Ibid.

[320] Ibid.

[321] Ibid.

[322] Ibid., p.122-123

[323] Ibid., p. 123

[324] Ibid.

[325] Ibid.

program holder immediately as they enter the premises.[326] Signage technology is nothing uncommon in the world of shopping, yet when paired with facial identification and Big Data evaluation, it may aim at a specific consumer according to his or her prior purchasing history.[327] This implies that labeling and display monitors might show consumer-focused messaging or advertisements, highlighting particular goods or promotions that might be of relevance.[328]

Technologies that employ self-learning robots enable for the fulfillment of tasks or activities by modifying behavior to the surroundings.[329] A common method retailers employ robots in shops is to assist consumers to find what they desire.[330] It 2016, Lowe's utilized the LoweBot robot at its San Francisco stores.[331] LoweBot collects data to detect buying patterns for a specific region, including seasonal and day-of-week trends.[332] Customers' desire to see them in operation enables retail robots to become a powerful tool for brand adoption and CE improvement.[333] Predictive analytics technology helps huge firms predict future customer behavior based on historical or current patterns, allowing for more informed strategic decisions.[334] Predictive analytics can help reduce customer turnover and identify risk scenarios.[335] Sephora, Under Armour, and Urban Outfitters use Dynamic Yield's strong ML engine to segment their customers.[336]

Mahmoud, Tehseen, and Fuxman (2020) suggest that AI can help shops enhance performance by identifying new income streams and implementing successful CRM methods.[337] AI streamlines repetitive sales processes, functions as a digital assistant, dynamically segments customers, and allows for individualized offerings.[338] The Pepper robot exemplifies how AI may enhance retail traffic, customer relationships, and sales revenue. Coversica, an AI-powered sales assistant, improves consumer connections by engaging in direct conversations[339]. Boch Automotive, a car dealer in New England, reported increased Toyota sales through the use of technology.[340]

---

[326] Ibid.

[327] Ibid.

[328] Ibid.

[329] Ibid.

[330] Ibid.

[331] Ibid.

[332] Ibid.

[333] Ibid.

[334] Ibid.

[335] Ibid.

[336] Ibid.

[337] Mahmoud, Ali B., Shehnaz Tehseen, and Leonora Fuxman. "The dark side of artificial intelligence in retail innovation." In Retail futures, p 171. Emerald Publishing Limited, 2020.

[338] Ibid.

[339] Ibid.

[340] Ibid.

AI is transforming how merchants manage their interactions with digital media.[341] RedBalloon, an Australian online gift business, employs Albert, an AI-powered platform, to provide personalized experiences.[342] Albert engages markets by combining artistic assets, acquiring advertisements, and conducting initiatives on premium as well as free media platforms such as Facebook, Google, and YouTube.[343] RedBalloon experienced a 750% increase in Facebook engagements and a 1500% profit from its advertising expenditures.[344]

According to Minbiole (2025), no matter the size of the retailer, determining which AI technologies to prioritize and where to begin might be difficult.[345] However, there are numerous ways in which retailers are currently utilizing AI to provide measurable value and a meaningful return on investment (ROI).[346] According to research, for every \$1 invested in generative AI, the ROI is 3.7 times across industries and geographies (vs 3.5 times in 2024).[347] Top executives employing generative AI are seeing much larger returns, with an average ROI of \$10.30—nearly three times greater.[348]

There are speculations that self-checkouts at chain retailers are encouraging shoplifting. According to Matyszczyk (2024), supermarkets have been spending heavily in self-checkout technology for some time.[349] This technique was very obvious.[350] It seemed to be an intelligent decision, something which would eliminate a necessity for numerous employees while also helping to reduce costs, which is essential for a low-margin sales operation.[351] However, the pragmatic application of self-checkout technologies has been less impressive.[352] While some customers like the option to breeze through the self-checkout lines without having to speak with someone, others have

---

[341] Ibid., p. 172

[342] Ibid.

[343] Ibid.

[344] Ibid.

[345] Minbiole, Anya. "More Human-Centered Retail with AI." Microsoft Industry Blogs, April 10, 2025. https://www.microsoft.com/en-us/industry/blog/retail/2025/04/10/more-human-centered-retail-with-ai/.

[346] Ibid.

[347] Ibid.

[348] Ibid.

[349] Matyszczyk, Chris. "Not Always Honest at Supermarket Self-Checkout? AI Is out to Get You." ZDNET, February 24, 2024. https://www.zdnet.com/article/not-always-honest-at-supermarket-self-checkout-ai-is-out-to-get-you/.

[350] Ibid.

[351] Ibid.

[352] Ibid.

been angry.[353] One Rhode Island legislator even attempted to pass legislation prohibiting stores from having too many self-checkout lanes operating at any given time.[354] The legislator feels she should not be required to do the same duties as a human employee.[355]

Target has also chosen to restrict self-checkout hours at select locations in an attempt to prevent the types of losses that other grocery companies have recorded at self-checkout machines.[356] Apparently, dishonest buyers are to blame for the losses.[357] The so-called shrink (losses caused by products not being paid for) may be up to 16 times higher at self-checkouts compared to cashier-operated lanes.[358] Diebold Nixdorf's AI-powered software suite, which would be available in 2024, would significantly reduce nonpayment.[359] The 'Vynamic Smart Vision | Shrink Reduction' software package interacts with an employee using a smartphone or tablet.[360] The technology combines multiple bits of software.[361] One program automatically detects an alcohol buyer's age, another asserts it can instantaneously discriminate between vegetable and fruit products, which is a major source of aggravation for many clients, and a third performs some police work.[362]

According to Tsirulnik (2025), self-checkout (SCO) has advanced beyond an effort to reduce costs to a key driver for contemporary retail.[363] The desire of consumers for rapid service and ease has led retailers to quickly use SCO technology to expedite processes and lessen reliance on personnel.[364] Nevertheless, this transition has revealed flaws, especially with theft and fraudulent activity.[365] Today, retailers face a significant loss prevention dilemma, as self-checkout shrink has increased dramatically because of causes such as barcode swapping, non-scans, and organized retail crime (ORC).[366] Conventional safety measures like human audits, periodic inspections and surveillance footage are

---

[353] Ibid.
[354] Ibid.
[355] Ibid.
[356] Ibid.
[357] Ibid.
[358] Ibid.
[359] Ibid.
[360] Ibid.
[361] Ibid.
[362] Ibid.
[363] Tsirulnik, Yevgeni. "How to Harness AI and Automation for Smarter Self-Checkout Security." Forbes, March 18, 2025. https://www.forbes.com/councils/forbestechcouncil/2025/03/18/the-future-of-self-checkout-harnessing-ai-and-automation-for-smarter-security/.

[364] Ibid.
[365] Ibid.
[366] Ibid.

less adequate to combat the increasing sophistication of fraudulent strategies.[367]

The retail sector is currently at an impasse, and AI and automation remains critical to protecting self-checkout situations.[368] AI-powered detection of fraud, immediate data analysis, and edge-based safety measures are reshaping the way merchants protect transactions while maintaining the user experience.[369] Although certain fraud is unintentional, such as mis-scans or bagging oversights, planned techniques like as barcode switching and "pass-around" fraud are becoming increasingly complex.[370] With self-checkout stations on increasing popularity, merchants need to transition away from conventional monitoring to AI-powered loss avoidance that improves protection while preserving customer satisfaction.[371] Conventional loss mitigation approaches, including human audits and surveillance footage, are unfortunately no longer effective to tackle complex self-checkout fraud.[372] Retailers are moving beyond reactive security and integrating fraud protection straight into the checkout process.[373] Image recognition allows continuous surveillance by identifying barcode swapping, product misplacement, and unscanned items sans operator involvement.[374] Edge AI processing enables rapid identification of fraud at the device threshold, eliminating latencies and lowering dependence on cloud-based solutions.[375] Intelligent sensors for weight ensure that scanned objects match its estimated size, preventing widespread mis-scanning fraud.[376]

I was in the Washington, DC, area in late 2023. I have used self-checkouts at retailers such as Target and Walmart. The DC area (including some Northern Virginia areas) has imposed a five-cent bag tax, which shoppers must honestly answer before paying. The proceeds from the bag tax goes to clean up the Anacostia River. For the Northern Virginia bag tax, proceeds go to clean up local wildlife.

According to Adanyin (2024), justice in AI assures all customers receive treatment fairly, regardless of race, gender, age, or other attributes.[377] With the retail sector, justice means that AI-

---

[367] Ibid.
[368] Ibid.
[369] Ibid.
[370] Ibid.
[371] Ibid.
[372] Ibid.
[373] Ibid.
[374] Ibid.
[375] Ibid.
[376] Ibid.
[377] Adanyin, Anthonette. "Ethical AI in Retail: Consumer Privacy and Fairness." *European Journal of Computer Science and Information Technology* 12, no. 7 (October 27, 2024): p. 24. https://doi.org/10.37745/ejcsit.2013/vol12n72135.

driven actions, including customized suggestions, costs, and customer profiles, do not discriminate against or perpetuate existing socioeconomic inequalities.[378] Store AI systems, including ones utilized for customized advertising or costs, need an objective.[379] Yet, AI systems taught on inaccurate information may continue unjust behavior; so, merchants must tackle computational prejudice and guarantee that AI methods for making decisions are clear and fair.[380] AI systems must be constantly monitored to guarantee that they do not unfairly disfavor specific categories of users.[381] Fairness is essential for sustaining a varied consumer base, avoiding legal issues, and upholding ethics.[382]

Accountability refers to businesses' responsibility to ensure ethical AI operations.[383] In retail, corporations must accept responsibility for their AI systems' actions and outputs, and address any negative effects, such as bias or data exploitation.[384] To maintain consumer trust, retailers should establish explicit methods for monitoring and addressing AI-related issues.[385]

Transparency is critical to building confidence in AI-powered retail operations.[386] Customers should comprehend how their information is employed, how AI generates judgments, and how it affects how they make their purchases.[387] Shops ought to give straightforward and readily available details on how AI systems work, such as data collection and personalized recommendations.[388] Transparency can reduce customer fears about AI's impact on their purchasing experiences and increase trust.[389]

Explainability is directly associated with transparency.[390] AI systems should be built to provide clear explanations for their actions.[391] Retail AI systems should explain why they recommend products or alter prices based on user behavior.[392] Clear information regarding AI decision-making processes can boost customer confidence in their fairness and accuracy.[393]

---

[378] Ibid.
[379] Ibid.
[380] Ibid.
[381] Ibid.
[382] Ibid., p. 24-25
[383] Ibid., p. 25
[384] Ibid.
[385] Ibid.
[386] Ibid.
[387] Ibid.
[388] Ibid.
[389] Ibid.
[390] Ibid.
[391] Ibid.
[392] Ibid.
[393] Ibid.

Explainability is directly associated with transparency.[394] AI systems should be built to provide clear explanations for their actions.[395] Retail AI systems should explain why they recommend products or alter prices based on user behavior.[396] Clear information regarding AI decision-making processes can boost customer confidence in their fairness and accuracy.[397]

Ghai (2024) defines sensor fusion as the combination of data from various sensors in order to improve the precision and dependability of self-checkout machines.[398] These systems can reliably track and verify purchases through the integration of data from photographic equipment, weight sensors, and radio frequency identification (RFID) chips.[399] AiFi's automated shop systems utilize a collection of sensors and cameras to monitor consumer movements and item engagements.[400] The use of this equipment allows for immediate control of inventory and provides significant understanding of consumer behavior and product interactions.[401] The coordinated collection of various data from sensors reduces inefficiencies and increases the reliability of the system[402] For instance, if the camera cannot identify a product due to a blockage, weight sensors can confirm the item's existence, assuring proper invoicing.[403]

According to Rigner (2019), AI Retailer Systems is a retail-focused start-up with a long-term goal of automating the shopping experience.[404] Automating the retail checkout method is not a new concept; it has existed since the 1980s and has performed in many ways, the most prominent being the self-scanning option.[405] Self-scanning eliminates the requirement for a cashier at each checkout point.[406] However, this needs the retail outlet to place trust in their consumers, trusting that they will scan all of the things they bring out of the store.[407]

---

[394] Ibid.

[395] Ibid.

[396] Ibid.

[397] Ibid.

[398] Ghai, Neha. "Grocery Doppio AI Disruptors: 5 Tech Innovators Revolutionizing Autonomous Checkout Systems." AI Innovators Revolutionizing Autonomous Checkout, November 4, 2024. https://www.grocerydoppio.com/articles/ai-innovators-autonomous-checkout.

[399] Ibid.

[400] Ibid.

[401] Ibid.

[402] Ibid.

[403] Ibid.

[404] Rigner, Anton. "AI-Based Machine Vision for Retail Self-Checkout System," 2019., p. 1

[405] Ibid.

[406] Ibid.

[407] Ibid.

Meghani and Sinha (2023) found that self-checkout systems increase the consumer experience by allowing for more control and freedom.[408] Self-service caters to varied client preferences, including those who value quick checkout and minimal interaction.[409] Customers often take less than four minutes before checking out using a self-checkout system, leading to a more efficient shopping experience.[410]

According to Ghazwani (2021), shopping is an essential part of people's everyday lives.[411] Marketing professionals, supervisors, and rival businesses strive to deliver an interesting and pleasant purchasing experience for consumers through advances that increase the quickness and effectiveness of their products and services.[412] Smart stores are a new, big invention that companies hope to establish in order to provide a more enjoyable shopping experience for customers while increasing revenues for businesses.[413] Amazon opened its first cashierless store on January 22, 2018.[414] The "Just Walk Out" technology simplifies the shopping experience by reducing the need for customers to wait in lines, interact with others, and carry cash.[415]

According to Adebakin (2023), because of the COVID-19 epidemic, merchants, particularly convenience stores, have implemented self-checkout technology.[416] During the pandemic, 87% of people preferred to buy in businesses with self-checkout options, especially touchless ones, which explains the rapid uptake.[417] The COVID-19 epidemic has prompted individuals and organizations to adapt to the new standards and practices, including social distancing and contactless encounters.[418] Self-checkout technology has become a popular option during the pandemic as it allows for speedy transactions with minimum connection with others.[419]

---

[408] Meghani, Manisha, and Hemlata Sinha. "Revolutionizing Retail: Design and Implementation of an AI-Powered Autonomous Checkout System." *International Journal on Recent and Innovation Trends in Computing and Communication* 11, no. 9 (September 30, 2023): p. 4929.

[409] Ibid.

[410] Ibid.

[411] Ghazwani, Salman. "The Impact of AI-Enabled Checkouts on Shoppers' Attitudes and Purchase Intent in Saudi Arabia," 2021., p. 2

[412] Ibid.

[413] Ibid.

[414] Ibid.

[415] Ibid.

[416] Adebakin, Adeyinka, and Jasmin Shokoui. "Self-Checkout for what? An Exploration of the Usage and Adoption of Self-Checkouts Before and After the COVID-19 Pandemic."

[417] Ibid.

[418] Ibid.

[419] Ibid.

According to Fãlco, et al. (2021), physical stores account for 90% of total retail sales.[420] In these physical stores, 40% of customers depart due to the wait time.[421] Autonomous retailers can reduce client wait times by issuing a receipt without scanning the items.[422] Previous approaches have focused solely on computer vision, combined it with weight sensors, or combined it with human product recognition.[423] Low accuracy, hour-long receipt generation delays, and inability to adapt to store-level installations because of computation needs and practical consumer circumstances.[424]

Giroux, et al. (2022) report that self-service technology and AI have impacted the retail sector by altering customer behavior and the whole process of shopping.[425] While AI brings incredible benefits for organizations, corporations must be aware of the perils and risks involved with the use of these systems.[426] Ethical intention (the intent of disclosing a mistake) is not as common to occur in AI and self-checkout devices than in traditional checkout.[427] Furthermore, ethical intention declines as individuals perceive the equipment as much less anthropomorphic.[428] The drop in morality is driven by a reduction in guilt toward new technologies.[429] The interaction's nonhuman nature diminishes feelings of guilt and, as a result, moral behavior.[430]

---

[420] Falcão, João Diogo, Carlos Ruiz, Adeola Bannis, Hae Young Noh, and Pei Zhang. "ISACS: In-Store Autonomous Checkout System for Retail." *Proceedings of the ACM on Interactive, Mobile, Wearable and Ubiquitous Technologies* 5, no. 3 (September 9, 2021): p. 1. https://doi.org/10.1145/3478086.

[421] Ibid.
[422] Ibid.
[423] Ibid.
[424] Ibid.
[425] Giroux, Marilyn, Jungkeun Kim, Jacob C. Lee, and Jongwon Park. "Artificial Intelligence and Declined Guilt: Retailing Morality Comparison between Human and AI." *Journal of Business Ethics* 178, no. 4 (February 12, 2022): p. 1027. https://doi.org/10.1007/s10551-022-05056-7.

[426] Ibid.
[427] Ibid.
[428] Ibid.
[429] Ibid.
[430] Ibid.

3 FUTURE OF BARBER SHOPS AND SALONS

I would only go to a stylist who is familiar with my hair and does his or her job. I have seen videos on social media that robots could take over the trade. I am apprehensive of a robot doing my hair. Common sense entails that electricity and water do not mix, so the Robo-Stylist would cause a shock if it washed my hair in the shampoo bowl.

Some people want to save time by cutting their own hair. Kyosuke, Terada, and Tsukamoto (2014) identified two major challenges for self-haircutting.[431] One environmental challenge is creating a suitable setting for self-haircutting.[432] Another challenge is mastering self-haircutting skills to get desired hairstyles.[433]

According to Guinness (2023), a robot hairdresser can make small talk while on the job.[434] Shane Wighton, a YouTuber and engineer, invented the robot because he disliked how traditional hairdressers performed.[435] He had to teach his robot to separate portions of hair and then cut them, which he accomplished with a tube that sucked it up one section at a time.[436]

---

[431] Kyosuke, Futami, Tsutomu Terada, and Masahiko Tsukamoto. "A System for Supporting Self-Haircuts Using Camera Equipped Robot." *Proceedings of the 12th International Conference on Advances in Mobile Computing and Multimedia*, December 8, 2014, p. 34. https://doi.org/10.1145/2684103.2684143.

[432] Ibid.

[433] Ibid.

[434] Guinness, Emma. "Man Creates Robot That Can Cut Hair Automatically." UNILAD, March 12, 2023. https://www.unilad.com/technology/man-creates-robot-cuts-hair-automatically-893468-20230312.

[435] Ibid.

[436] Ibid.

According to Burton (2020), Whigton created the robot during the COVID-19 epidemic as a quarantine haircut technique.[437] The robot employs a computer algorithm that provides various haircut styles.[438] The robot's scissors are hooked to an adjustable lever that spins around its head.[439] To ensure safety, the robot assesses the distance between the hair it wishes to clip and the scalp.[440] As a result, the robot was unable to make cuts around Wighton's ears.[441] Then, similar to the iconic Flowbee haircutting machine from the 1980s, the vacuum system within the automated device pulls the hair tight.[442] The device chooses the hair to be clipped, and then uses the robot's associated scissors.[443] The end results were interesting.[444] Wighton's haircut was not spectacular, but it was not bad either.[445] The only other disadvantage of his robot is that it appears to take significantly longer to cut hair than a human barber.[446]

Yoo, et al. (2025) propose haircut robots may tackle constraints on labor in nursing homes and assisted living facilities and allow individuals with restricted mobility to maintain their hairstyle-related personality.[447] MOE-Hair is a gentle robotic device that can execute three haircare duties: scalp massage, hand combing, and hair gripping.[448] The device combines a tendon-driven delicate robot end-effector (MOE) along with a wrist-mounted RGBD camera, that utilizes combined hydraulic adherence for protection and optical pressure sensing via deformation.[449] In power-sensorized mannequin hair testing, MOE obtained equivalent hair-grasping performance despite using significantly less power compared to inflexible gripping devices.[450] An improved force estimating approach that combines optical distortion information with actuator ligament stresses reduces detection inaccuracies by as much as 60.1% and 20.3%, respectively, compared to baselines based just on actuator current load and depth images.[451]

---

[437] Burton, Bonnie. "This Robot Will Give You a New Haircut... If You Dare." CNET, July 22, 2020. https://www.cnet.com/science/this-robot-will-give-you-a-new-haircut-if-you-dare/.

[438] Ibid.
[439] Ibid.
[440] Ibid.
[441] Ibid.
[442] Ibid.
[443] Ibid.
[444] Ibid.
[445] Ibid.
[446] Ibid.
[447] Yoo, Uksang, Nathaniel Dennler, Eliot Xing, Maja Mataric, Stefanos Nikolaidis, Jeffrey Ichnowski, and Jean Oh. "Soft and Compliant Contact-Rich Hair Manipulation and Care." *arXiv preprint arXiv:2501.02630*, January 5, 2025, p. 1.

[448] Ibid.
[449] Ibid.
[450] Ibid.
[451] Ibid.

Hair influences people's identities and self-esteem.[452] Notably, as people become older, the relevance of hair to their self-esteem grows.[453] As we age and lose movement, caring for our hair becomes a time-consuming and challenging daily activity.[454] It additionally essential to individual cleanliness.[455] Regardless, the majority of elderly care and hospice facilities depend primarily on volunteer barbers and stylists to provide haircare services.[456] To overcome the shortfall in hair-care services, researchers proposed using robots to assist with combing.[457] Previous studies found that humans often regard inflexible robots as "rough."[458] Robots face a perception issue when performing hair care and manipulation jobs, as hair can obscure the underlying scalp, making it impossible to apply constant force on the head using only exterior vision.[459]

Soft robot manipulators offer numerous advantages when interacting with humans.[460] Their compliance renders them secure in chaotic conditions and greater resilience in contact-intensive handling professions.[461] Gentle manipulators for robots are especially beneficial for physical interaction human-robot interaction (pHRI) applications.[462] Humans consider soft robots as safer than rigid counterparts.[463] Soft robot manipulators flex upon contact, unlike stiff robots.[464] Watching these distortions suggests a possible approach to employ soft robots in participatory awareness.[465]

Robots are increasingly competent of assisting people with various activities of daily living (ADLs).[466] Feeding, washing, and dressing were among the applications investigated.[467] Hair care, like other ADLs, was judged by participants to be vital for retaining well-being and dignity.[468] Because hair grooming and care are labor-intensive processes, automated and robotic alternatives have been

---

[452] Ibid.
[453] Ibid.
[454] Ibid.
[455] Ibid.
[456] Ibid.
[457] Ibid.
[458] Ibid.
[459] Ibid.
[460] Ibid., p. 1-2
[461] Ibid., p. 2
[462] Ibid.
[463] Ibid.
[464] Ibid.
[465] Ibid.
[466] Ibid.
[467] Ibid.
[468] Ibid.

proposed.[469] Previous research on haircare robotics concentrated on physically assessing hair circulation and alternatively maintaining current hair circulation patterns or employing a specific sensorized hairbrush and an input processor that included a high-fidelity pressure detector linked with an end-effector.[470]

According to Sepenu and Eliasen (2022), cosmetics and beauty items have been used from ancient times in Egypt, Rome, and Greece.[471] Archaeological evidence reveals that Neanderthals used brown, red, and yellow arsenic, clay, and mud as the earliest types of cosmetics.[472] Hair was also applied on bones to curl, and tattoos, cosmetics, and accessories were utilized to represent position and status.[473] Cold cream was devised by an ancient Greek physician named Galen, while the Romans employed petroleum-based scents and smells within their baths, fountains, and all over their bodies in order to assist people in unwinding and alleviate stress.[474] As migration and commerce increased in the 13th century, entrepreneurs introduced fragrances from the Far East into Europe, revitalizing the business.[475] The beauty and cosmetics sector has a considerable impact on regional and national economies across the globe.[476] Payments, service support, and the payment of wages and taxes all contribute to considerable wealth and employment creation that benefits both residents and countries alike.[477] This industry's production and ancillary services have a significant impact on many other industries. [478]

HairCo distributes professional hair care products primarily to salons and stylists.[479] HairCo faces hurdles as they lack direct access to consumer data, resulting in limited advertising initiatives to reach this demographic.[480] HairCo's impact mostly affects salons and stylists, who then propose goods to consumers.[481] Salon or stylist sales data can provide insights into the final consumer, but it cannot be

---

[469] Ibid.

[470] Ibid.

[471] Sepenu, Alexander K, and Linda Eliasen. "A Machine Learning Approach to Revenue Generation within the A Machine Learning Approach to Revenue Generation within the Professional Hair Care Industry Professional Hair Care Industry." *SMU Data Science Review* 6, no. 1 (Spring 2022): p. 1.

[472] Ibid.

[473] Ibid.

[474] Ibid.

[475] Ibid.

[476] Ibid.

[477] Ibid.

[478] Ibid.

[479] Ibid.

[480] Ibid.

[481] Ibid.

directly identify them because of professional standards of conduct regulations.[482]

Without AI technology, sales have dropped.[483] HairCo is looking to use ML models to increase profits and reduce client attrition.[484] HairCo would focus on grouping and regression to achieve its ML aims.[485] Customer clustering, also known as segmentation, is the process of categorizing a company's customers into various groups based on characteristics and important indicators.[486] The cluster's data points share similar traits but differ from those in other clusters.[487] ML algorithms reveal insights and groups that firms may not discover on their own, laying the framework for establishing consumer profiles and identifying high revenue-generating customers.[488] This helps HairCo identify the most effective client engagement strategies for each category.[489] Marketers can create personalized client profiles for every category, to tailor marketing campaigns according to their unique wants and traits.[490] This can lead to increased product sales through persuasive advertising.[491] The sales prediction model identifies the most significant elements influencing revenue.[492] This intelligence can inform strategic planning and improve resource allocation and marketing initiatives.[493] This approach enables sales teams to prioritize high-value offers, resulting in higher-quality revenue.[494] Tailored strategies aim to increase consumer value, drive loyalty, and ensure market stability.[495]

According to Square (2024), the stylist's chair can serve as a gathering place for trading stories and catching up on current events or gossip.[496] However, addressing AI and how beauty businesses use it to develop is not typical shop conversation.[497] Whether one owns the most opulent spa or the smallest barbershop, AI-powered technology is certainly already making (or has the potential to

---

[482] Ibid.

[483] Ibid., p. 2

[484] Ibid.

[485] Ibid.

[486] Ibid.

[487] Ibid.

[488] Ibid.

[489] Ibid.

[490] Ibid.

[491] Ibid.

[492] Ibid.

[493] Ibid.

[494] Ibid.

[495] Ibid.

[496] Square. "AI in the Beauty Industry: Square." The Bottom Line by Square, October 29, 2024. https://squareup.com/us/en/the-bottom-line/operating-your-business/ai-beauty-industry.

[497] Ibid.

make) the styling industry more efficient and customers happier.[498]

According to Frye (2025), AI is altering the way people work and live, and the beauty and wellness business is no exception.[499] As customer expectations shift and competition heats up, firms must move beyond expertise and imagination to stay ahead of the curve.[500] AI enables organizations to fulfill escalating customer demands while freeing up time to focus on what is most important: providing amazing experiences that keep clients coming back.[501] The salon and spa industry relies heavily on personal customer contacts and strong connections.[502] Calls may go unanswered while the stylist is busy, potentially costing her bookings and new clients.[503] Here's where AI comes in to aid. Mindbody's virtual receptionist, Messenger[AI], ensures that every call is captured and every client is attended to, regardless of time of day.[504] The AI-powered chatbot is available 24/7 and employs individualized interactions based on each client's preferences and previous interactions to provide a seamless and engaging experience.[505] It does more than just handle missed calls; it can check staff schedules, arrange appointments, and securely process payments by text, all while allowing for easy communication between the stylist and clients.[506] With Messenger[ai] taking care of these responsibilities, the stylist can focus on strengthening customer connections and expanding the business.[507] AI improves reporting and analytics for spas and salons by transforming data into meaningful insights that drive better decisions.[508] The stylist can use AI-powered tools to track performance data including as client retention rates, average spend per visit, and the popularity of various services.[509] These techniques can also assist stylists analyze trends in client behavior, such as peak booking periods or seasonal service preferences, allowing them to optimize staffing and promotions.[510]

AI can improve inventory management in salons and spas by allowing stylists to effortlessly

---

[498] Ibid.

[499] Frye, Ma-Keba. "How Can AI Help You Grow Your Salon and Spa Business?" Mindbody, March 11, 2025.
https://www.mindbodyonline.com/business/education/blog/what-ai-and-how-can-it-help-you-grow-your-salon-and-spa-business.

[500] Ibid.
[501] Ibid.
[502] Ibid.
[503] Ibid.
[504] Ibid.
[505] Ibid.
[506] Ibid.
[507] Ibid.
[508] Ibid.
[509] Ibid.
[510] Ibid.

monitor inventory levels in real time, ensuring that vital supplies never run out or surplus products go unused.[511] These systems use sales patterns and customer preferences to estimate demand, allowing stylists to stock the correct supplies at the right time.[512] AI also makes reordering easier by automatically informing the stylist when supplies run short or it's time to refill popular goods.[513] This streamlined strategy saves time, lowers waste, and increases profits.[514]

Client retention is easier to manage and negotiate when the stylist anticipates his or her client's demands and actions.[515] AI can assist stylists in analyzing client data, including as appointment frequency, missed reservations, and time since their previous visit, to identify clients who may not return.[516] Using AI, it identifies clients and members who are likely to miss lessons or appointments, providing insights and the opportunity to help before they leave permanently.[517] Once marked, the stylist can contact them by phone call, tailored text, or email messages to encourage reengagement.[518] These communications could contain unique deals or heartfelt sentiments like "We miss you!"[519] By reaching out at the proper moment with a targeted approach, the stylist may strengthen relationships with his or her clients and keep them returning.[520]

AI appointment scheduling solutions streamline salon and spa bookings by assessing historical behaviors, provider availability, and customer preferences.[521] These systems leverage historical booking data to identify appropriate appointment times, reducing scheduling gaps and increasing productivity for stylists and other personnel.[522] Furthermore, AI helps automated online booking systems by allowing clients to simply check available appointments, set their chosen time, and receive reminders.[523] This not only saves time, but improves the whole client experience.[524]

According to Skinner (2023), AI can assist in the creation of advertising materials for beauty

---

[511] Ibid.
[512] Ibid.
[513] Ibid.
[514] Ibid.
[515] Ibid.
[516] Ibid.
[517] Ibid.
[518] Ibid.
[519] Ibid.
[520] Ibid.
[521] Ibid.
[522] Ibid.
[523] Ibid.
[524] Ibid.

salons as well as social media content.[525] AI-powered content generators, such as ChatGPT or Smartwriter.ai, can help the stylist develop fascinating and engaging content for social media, blog articles, and other advertising materials.[526] Furthermore, AI can be utilized to generate advertising graphics and films automatically (Midjourney, Lexica, Looka, Images.AI, among others).[527] Some systems, for example, can automatically generate photographs or films displaying new items or services, saving time while also boosting the visual attractiveness of the salon's marketing materials.[528]

Torres, et al. (2024) report that eyelash extensions are a popular beauty trend that enhances natural attractiveness and personal style.[529] Eyelash extensions are a transformational option to achieve stunning, fluttering lashes that fascinate and ooze charm.[530] Eyelash extensions provide volume, length, and curl to real lashes through painstakingly application of individual synthetic lashes.[531] Lash experts expertly design extensions to fit each individual's eye shape and desired style.[532] Eyelash extensions can enhance the eyes and frame the face in various ways, from subtle to dramatic.[533] Eyelash extensions have been increasingly popular in recent decades, overcoming barriers in gender, age, and culture.[534] The attractiveness of these products rests not only in their immediate visual benefits, but also in their convenience in regular beauty procedures.[535] Lash extensions eliminates the need for mascara and artificial lashes, resulting in a beautiful and hassle-free appearance.[536] Lash extensions are a popular way to enhance natural attractiveness and express one's distinctive personality.[537] Lash salons are popular among individuals looking for long, lustrous lashes.[538] Choosing appropriate lash styles, scheduling appointments, and finding quality salons may be challenging for both consumers and salon workers.[539]

---

[525] Skinner, Andy. "Artificial Intelligence (AI) in Beauty Industry." EasyWeek, April 10, 2023. https://easyweek.io/artificial-intelligence-in-beauty-industry.html.

[526] Ibid.

[527] Ibid.

[528] Ibid.

[529] Torres, Allen Jasfer Gaspado, Mathew Lizardo Flores, Catherine Ann Pilapil, and Criselle Jose Centeno. "Lash Tech: A Web App-Based Lash Recommendation, Virtual Try-on, and Seamless Booking App Using GEO Location Powered by Artificial Intelligence." *Journal of Electrical Systems* 20, no. 5s (April 2024): p. 1118. https://doi.org/10.52783/jes.2424.

[530] Ibid.

[531] Ibid.

[532] Ibid.

[533] Ibid.

[534] Ibid.

[535] Ibid.

[536] Ibid.

[537] Ibid.

[538] Ibid.

[539] Ibid., p. 1118-1119

To solve these issues, the researchers created an application for smartphones with AI-powered eyelash advise and digital eyelash try-on, a streamlined scheduling structure, and a salon site.[540] The AI-powered eyelash suggestion system analyzes customers' facial characteristics and eye dimensions precisely.[541] Through evaluating the above facial information, the algorithm creates tailored eyelash suggestions that suit each person's distinctive appearance.[542] The digital eyelash try-on tool enables customers to see different eyelash dimensions, curls, and densities in instantaneously.[543] The smartphone application has an easy scheduling mechanism which enables customers to book eyelash sessions instantly via the application.[544] Lastly, the smartphone application would include a local eyelash salon finder to boost user convenience and provide simple accessibility to nearby eyelash establishments.[545] An appointment reminder function helps clients keep on track with lash maintenance by sending timely alerts, eliminating missed appointments.[546]

The idea for developing the LashTech online application stemmed from the need to confront and solve issues in the lash sector.[547] Customers have difficulty with choosing acceptable lash designs lacking a visual aid, hindering their ability to make decisions.[548] Manual scheduling leads to bottlenecks and appointment cancellations, significantly impacting the entire customer satisfaction experience.[549] Clients struggle to find local quality lash salons without a specific geolocation software.[550] LashTech aims to improve the eyelash beauty experience by providing a straightforward digital try-on, a computerized scheduling structure, and location features.[551]

According to Türkal (2024), technology and innovation influence every business, including barbering.[552] With the rise of AI, barber supplies have seen a radical transition, making barbers' jobs easier and more efficient.[553] Among the basic advantages of AI in barbershops is its possibility to

---

[540] Ibid., p. 1119
[541] Ibid.
[542] Ibid.
[543] Ibid.
[544] Ibid.
[545] Ibid.
[546] Ibid.
[547] Ibid.
[548] Ibid.
[549] Ibid.
[550] Ibid.
[551] Ibid.
[552] Türkal, Barış. "The Impact of Artificial Intelligence on Barbering." BarberSets, February 7, 2024. https://barbersets.com/blogs/blogs/the-impact-of-artificial-intelligence-on-barbering.

[553] Ibid.

enhance precision and accuracy.[554] AI-powered barber tools, such clippers and trimmers, are intended to deliver a uniform and exact cut every time.[555] These products employ powerful algorithms to identify and change cutting length based on the user's preferred style.[556] This saves time while also ensuring that the customer receives a high-quality haircut.[557] AI can also help barbers make cutting-edge hairdo recommendations to their clients.[558] AI algorithms can recommend the best hairstyles for a person based on their face traits, hair texture, and previous haircut preferences.[559] This personalized recommendation system enables barbers to provide a more specialized and gratifying experience to their clients, hence increasing consumer happiness and loyalty.[560] AI has helped to bring virtual reality (VR) and augmented reality (AR) technology to the barbering industry.[561] Barbers can now create virtual barbering experiences for their customers, allowing them to see numerous hairstyles and colors before making a decision.[562] This immersive technology allows buyers to try on different styles without committing, making the transaction entertaining and exciting.[563] AI systems have made considerable advances in evaluating hair and scalp issues.[564] Barbers may now employ AI-powered gadgets to assess the health of the hair and scalp, identify potential problems like dandruff or hair loss, and offer appropriate treatments or solutions.[565] This comprehensive hair analysis enables barbers to provide personalized solutions to their clients and solve specific hair difficulties successfully.[566]

According to Hubal (2024), consider having a digital assistant who not only monitors the barber's clientele but also effortlessly analyzes their behaviors and preferences.[567] Barberly created a client profile application called the 'Love Story' feature, which comes into action.[568] This feature, designed to provide barbers with full customer profiles, consolidates critical information into a single, simple-

---

[554] Ibid.

[555] Ibid.

[556] Ibid.

[557] Ibid.

[558] Ibid.

[559] Ibid.

[560] Ibid.

[561] Ibid.

[562] Ibid.

[563] Ibid.

[564] Ibid.

[565] Ibid.

[566] Ibid.

[567] Hubal, Nataliia. "Fuel Your Barbershop Growth with AI-Powered Client Insights." Barberly Help Center, 2024. https://help.barberly.com/en/articles/9486352-fuel-your-barbershop-growth-with-ai-powered-client-insights.

[568] Ibid.

to-use interface.[569] The direct messaging network integration such as WhatsApp into the client's profile facilitates interaction.[570] Whether it is providing appointment reminders or tailored updates, staying in touch with clients has never been simple.[571]

According to Allen, et al. (2023), increasing access to and engagement in computer science is critical at all education levels.[572] Nevertheless, an example that might restrict contemplating participation and accessibility is the computer science pipeline.[573] The concept of a pipeline frequently defines accessibility to and involvement in computer science using an unchanging procedure, therefore, could give rise to a limiting "one-size-fits-all" approach to promoting more accessible, varied, and welcoming kinds of learning.[574] It could be particularly relevant in initiatives to increase engagement beyond status, disability, color, and gender at both secondary and primary levels.[575]

The Barbershop Computing project focuses on significant connections between the cultural, historical, interpersonal, and technical features of African American barbers and barbershops in the United States.[576] They are avenues for motivation to those working to transform computer science instruction and learning.[577] It additionally caused people to reconsider the preconceptions concerning what is needed to increase accessibility and involvement in computer science.[578] Rather than rendering computer science accessible through a narrow path or a rigid algorithm, Barbershop Computing aims to develop multi-directional routes, communities with different expertise, and support networks at various scales—all with an objective of serving African American boys.[579] It shifts the objective of computer science education from limiting notions of technology employment readiness to more open and emerging ones.[580] Barbershop Computing is among the initiatives showcased within the Culturally Situated Design Tools website.[581] Additional

---

[569] Ibid.

[570] Ibid.

[571] Ibid.

[572] Allen, Madison C, Eleanor R. Glover Gladney, Michael Lachney, Marwin McKnight, Theodore S Ransaw, Dominick Sanders, and Aman Yadav. "Barbershop Computing." Communications of the ACM, October 1, 2023. https://cacm.acm.org/opinion/barbershop-computing/.

[573] Ibid.

[574] Ibid.

[575] Ibid.

[576] Ibid.

[577] Ibid.

[578] Ibid.

[579] Ibid.

[580] Ibid.

[581] Ibid.

endeavors include instructional resources and technological advances developed in conjunction with African American braiders, Indigenous artisans, fantasy writers, and others.[582] Rather than viewing culture as a glittering coating on "real" subject matter, the initiatives are built on the premise that diverse and pertinent learning materials can arise from cultural customs, concepts, and settings.[583] Actually, African American barbershops were previously associated with wealth creation and business, social conversation, connection construction, racial freedom, and cultural creation.[584] As a result, numerous barbers have become relied on locals, not only offering excellent haircuts and promoting wellness, but are occasionally involved with providing public health information, implementing literacy initiatives, promoting African American behavioral health accessibility, participating in civic engagement, and many other activities.[585]

---

[582] Ibid.

[583] Ibid.

[584] Ibid.

[585] Ibid.

4 AI IN FINANCES

According to Kaya, Schildbach, Schneider, and Deutsche Bank Attorney General (2019), banks are typically early adopters of information technology (IT) opportunities.[586] This applies not only to the rear office, where contemporary technology has long been deployed (for example, to handle transactions), but additionally to the front end of the company.[587] A prime instance is automated teller machines (ATMs), which were among the first IT uses in finance.[588] These tools eliminated bank stall repeated debits and account status monitoring.[589] They improved bank efficiency and made conventional financial services more accessible to customers.[590] When the first ATM was placed in London in 1967, they have grown ubiquitous in locations.[591] In Europe, there are now three ATMs per branch in 2017, compared to one per four in 1987.[592] Bank personnel may now focus on relationship banking, offering credit cards, loans, and investment products, as they are no longer required to handle cash.[593]

Online banking is another example of a bank implementing client-facing new IT.[594]
Since the late 1990s, internet banking has become increasingly popular.[595] Direct or internet banks

---

[586] Kaya, Orçun, Jan Schildbach, Deutsche Bank AG, and Stefan Schneider. "Artificial intelligence in banking." *Artificial intelligence* (2019) p. 4.
[587] Ibid.
[588] Ibid.
[589] Ibid.
[590] Ibid.
[591] Ibid.
[592] Ibid.
[593] Ibid.
[594] Ibid.
[595] Ibid.

with few or no physical branches have developed.[596] Almost all banks began offering online banking services.[597] In 2018, over 50% of adults in the EU utilized internet banking to monitor balances and move payments.[598] Denmark has an unusually high online banking penetration rate (90%).[599] In Germany, 59% of people used online banking in 2018, up from 35% in 2007.[600] Online banking has become the primary service option for clients with limited time to visit a branch.[601] The way bank clients access the internet has also evolved.[602] Germans are increasingly embracing mobile devices for internet banking, with 40% having a banking app installed.[603] Furthermore, one-fifth of the customers utilize their smartphone applications for mobile transactions.[604] This is especially common amongst younger, better educated, and online-savvy people.[605] Banks and customers are increasingly adopting online platforms and internet services, reducing the need for physical branches.[606]

According to O'Brien and Downie (2024), AI has grown into a growing crucial innovation for the financial services industry.[607] When used to power insider activities and client-facing programs, it can assist institutions strengthen client satisfaction, detect fraud, and manage assets and liabilities.[608] Traditionally, established banking organizations have experienced difficulties with innovation.[609] Large banks performed 40% less productively than digital natives.[610] Many emerging financial organizations are leading the way in AI applications, underlining the necessity for established banks to catch up and experiment.[611]

Investment banks have long employed natural language processing (NLP) to parse huge data volumes generated internally or obtained from external parties.[612] Firms use NLP to examine

---

596 Ibid.
597 Ibid.
598 Ibid.
599 Ibid.
600 Ibid.
601 Ibid.
602 Ibid.
603 Ibid.
604 Ibid.
605 Ibid.
606 Ibid.
607 O'Brien, Keith, and Amanda Downie. "What Is AI in Banking?" IBM, May 1, 2024. https://www.ibm.com/think/topics/ai-in-banking.

608 Ibid.
609 Ibid.
610 Ibid.
611 Ibid.
612 Ibid.

information sets and make more educated choices on critical financial decisions and money control.[613] The financial sector, in particular, is reaping the expected benefits of AI technologies.[614] Customers demand digital banking experiences: apps that allow them to learn more about the services offered, communicate with real people or virtual assistants, and better manage their money.[615] To keep customers satisfied, businesses must improve the user experience.[616] Adopting and deploying AI technology is one approach to do this.[617]

Financial services firms are adopting AI for various reasons, including risk management, client experience, and market trend predictions.[618] AI assists customers in making more informed financial decisions.[619] They are more likely to stick with banks that deploy cutting-edge AI technologies to assist them manage their money.[620] However, given the various industry rules, banks and other financial services businesses require a complete plan for handling AI.[621] To reduce risk and exposure, AI must be used in conjunction with a smart framework.[622]

According to Beck (2024), the AI application in the financial industry has substantially enhanced the client experience.[623] AI-powered technology, notably chatbots and sophisticated data analysis, has changed ways banks communicate with their clients, delivering previously unobtainable degrees of customization and reaction.[624] Several financial institutions now deploy AI-powered chatbots for customer service, providing speedy answers to customer queries and 24-hour support.[625] Since its launch in 2018, Bank of America's AI chatbot Erica has had over 1.5 billion engagements.[626] It provides support to customers around the clock, successfully processing inquiries and interactions, leading to lower delays and increased customer happiness.[627] Prior to

---

[613] Ibid.

[614] Ibid.

[615] Ibid.

[616] Ibid.

[617] Ibid.

[618] Ibid.

[619] Ibid.

[620] Ibid.

[621] Ibid.

[622] Ibid.

[623] Beck, Serge. "How Artificial Intelligence Is Reshaping Banking." Forbes, February 23, 2024.
https://www.forbes.com/councils/forbestechcouncil/2024/02/23/how-artificial-intelligence-is-reshaping-banking/.

[624] Ibid.

[625] Ibid.

[626] Ibid.

[627] Ibid.

2018, this has never happened in the financial sector.[628]

Banks currently use AI algorithms to monitor customer information, recognize certain financial transactions, and provide individualized advice.[629] This kind of customized focus empowers customers to make better fiscal choices, creates confidence, and increases client retention.[630] Barclays' application of AI for identifying fraudulent activity is a great example of the technology's capacity to enhance its client experience.[631] Their AI system monitors money transfers instantaneously, identifying and avoiding fraud.[632] This preemptive method not just safeguards clients but additionally builds confidence in the bank's safety procedures.[633] In a comparable manner Bank of America's Glass, an AI-powered evaluation tool, exemplifies the unique application of AI in finance.[634] Glass integrates market statistics with financial theories, using ML methods to discover business patterns and forecast customer demand.[635] This not only allows for personalized investment counseling, yet it also positions the banking organization as a leader in the application of AI for critical financial analysis.[636]

AI's innovation lies in its ability to acquire knowledge through interactions with users, continually modifying and enhancing its application layout to fit particular customers' developing interests and habits.[637] Thus, when an individual frequently examines their investment accounts, the AI may modify the mobile application's interface to emphasize particular financial characteristics, making them more accessible.[638] Similarly, when someone else frequently trades funds globally, the smartphone application might modify to showcase these features, so enhancing their financial journey.[639] This operates instantaneously.[640] The banking app's AI can examine each customer's everyday activities.[641] When a person opens his or her mobile bank app each day around 3 p.m. to move money, the AI could take note and rearrange the user interface to facilitate the process

---

[628] Ibid.
[629] Ibid.
[630] Ibid.
[631] Ibid.
[632] Ibid.
[633] Ibid.
[634] Ibid.
[635] Ibid.
[636] Ibid.
[637] Ibid.
[638] Ibid.
[639] Ibid.
[640] Ibid.
[641] Ibid.

quicker at the moment.[642]

This AI-driven personalization may extend past usefulness.[643] It may contain visible application characteristics like layouts, notification styles, and themes that are personalized to the customer's actions and likings.[644] As a user whom prefers a simple layout, the AI could simplify the user experience by eliminating distractions and stressing vital functionalities.[645] However, those who are intrigued in exact statistics and conclusions may benefit from the program's additional data-rich layout, which delivers specific economic data at their fingertips.[646] Banks and neobanks can employ AI to build an online setting which seems specifically suited for every consumer, instilling an atmosphere of comfort and convenience that improves the entire financial process.[647]

Sheth, et al. (2022) cite quick and flexible financial services, the requirement towards outstanding financial services, and worldwide estrangement as driving factors for the emergence of AI-mediated banking services.[648] AI mediation has significantly lowered everyday financial expenses, along with 1.6 times increase in effectiveness, when integrated into current gateways.[649] AI-mediated solutions are useful and suggested.[650] As future prosperity depends on personalized offers, financial products are likely to follow suit.[651]

While AI has revolutionized finance, it still has limitations.[652] Despite its appealing and charming character, AI has significant flaws.[653] According to recent studies, AI integration has a substantial impact on susceptible users in emerging markets.[654] Emerging markets differ significantly from developed nations.[655] The diverse user base makes it difficult for users to accept AI technology.[656]

---

[642] Ibid.
[643] Ibid.
[644] Ibid.
[645] Ibid.
[646] Ibid.
[647] Ibid.
[648] Sheth, Jagdish N., Varsha Jain, Gourav Roy, and Amrita Chakraborty. "AI-Driven Banking Services: The Next Frontier for a Personalized Experience in the Emerging Market." *International Journal of Bank Marketing* 40, no. 6 (July 20, 2022): p. 1248. https://doi.org/10.1108/ijbm-09-2021-0449.

[649] Ibid.
[650] Ibid.
[651] Ibid.
[652] Ibid., p. 1249
[653] Ibid.
[654] Ibid.
[655] Ibid.
[656] Ibid.

The absence of technical expertise has led to unexpected circumstances like digital theft, fraud, and money laundering.[657] Consumers questioned the reliability and legitimacy of AI in financial services.[658]

AI-powered financial products are unique and distinctive.[659] Nowadays, banks integrate AI-enabled technologies into their existing banking enterprise resource planning (ERP).[660] The incorporation of AI enablers benefits a financial institution in various ways.[661] AI employs clever algorithms to create tailored banking entrances for each individual client.[662] Furthermore, a personalized strategy allows a bank to deepen its relationship with its customers.[663] As a result, personalized banking services assist customers in performing important financial operations while also aiming to improve the financial services experience.[664] AI enables banking using official applications.[665] Once people use AI-enabled financial services, the AI begins to perceive their financial needs.[666] As a result, AI creates financial metrics for customers and places their service needs.[667] Overall, there are numerous uses for AI in banking services.[668] Banks have low reliance on technology.[669] Humans have primarily functioned as banking service gateways.[670] To address the limits of human support, advanced technology was used to improve banking services.[671] AI has revolutionized banking services, benefiting both banks and users.[672] Personalization enhances the convenience and efficiency of banking services.[673] AI enhances banks' service quality.[674] Technologically driven enterprises minimize service interruptions, obstacles, and mistakes made by humans.[675] AI enablers, which are non-volatile and based on higher programming languages, can assist banks and improve their services.[676]

---

[657] Ibid.
[658] Ibid.
[659] Ibid., p. 1250
[660] Ibid.
[661] Ibid.
[662] Ibid.
[663] Ibid.
[664] Ibid.
[665] Ibid.
[666] Ibid.
[667] Ibid.
[668] Ibid.
[669] Ibid.
[670] Ibid.
[671] Ibid.
[672] Ibid.
[673] Ibid.
[674] Ibid.
[675] Ibid.
[676] Ibid.

Although incorporating AI into financial services is critical, AI-enabled financial services can be complex.[677] Finally, enhanced amenities have the potential to improve both customer satisfaction and service quality.[678] While it is clear that AI-powered services are effective, recent research has raised some concerns.[679] AI-driven banking relies on algorithms rather than manual processes.[680] These financial applications use machine and programming languages.[681] As a result, operating these services requires experience and knowledge, which banks frequently lack.[682] A lack of technological expertise affects the user experience.[683] Users in emerging markets have diverse demographics, making the adoption of AI-centric services difficult and time-consuming.[684] The technological aspects of banking software frequently cause confusion among users.[685] Additionally, due to demographic disparities, some users may struggle to grasp English-based banking software.[686]

South Asian economies are vulnerable to online fraud and theft because of a diverse audience and predominantly rural culture.[687] Due to a lack of advanced banking skills, fraudsters can exploit the situation.[688] During the pandemic, India experienced the highest rate of digital fraud.[689] Using AI-centric tools requires a strong command of English.[690]

Traditional financial services were to be considered tedious; but, because of human engagement, customers trusted the services.[691] Despite being diverse and unique, AI enablers have struggled to explain their value to users.[692] When customers and management lack the necessary technical expertise, AI-powered products can harm banking.[693] Cyber theft is a widespread source

---

[677] Ibid., p. 1251
[678] Ibid.
[679] Ibid.
[680] Ibid.
[681] Ibid.
[682] Ibid.
[683] Ibid.
[684] Ibid.
[685] Ibid.
[686] Ibid.
[687] Ibid.
[688] Ibid.
[689] Ibid.
[690] Ibid.
[691] Ibid.
[692] Ibid.
[693] Ibid.

of fear today and individuals are increasingly sensitive to digital theft.[694] As a whole, the prospects for AI facilitators in financial institutions are highly bright.[695] However, the alarming conditions require major response.[696]

According to Oyeniyi, Ugochukwu, and Mhlongo (2024), the digitization of the financial services industry has raised customer standards.[697] Banks' use of virtual agents, such as chatbots, has not increased client engagement as intended.[698] This mismatch underlines the difficulties that banks confront in connecting their digital conversion activities with consumer preferences and expectations.[699] Furthermore, the use of AI in consumer support has considerably increased the effectiveness of those services.[700] Chatbots, in particular, have helped reduce lines at customer service centers, freeing up human employees to handle increasingly difficult issues.[701] This shift represents a larger pattern in the financial business of using AI to improve client relations.[702] Adopting AI tolls enables banks to address efficiency and personalization needs while also navigating digital transformation hurdles.[703] AI's impact on customer service methods is crucial as the banking industry evolves.[704] Banks must adapt to shifting consumer expectations and technology improvements.[705]

AI integration in banking has improved efficiency, personalized experiences, and problem-solving capabilities.[706] The advancements show the financial sector's dedication to using AI for future planning and operational excellence.[707] Integrating AI into banking brings hurdles, like guaranteeing transaction security and ethical implications.[708] The banking sector aims to use AI to build innovative, efficient, and customer-friendly products, despite the challenges of integrating it.[709] AI in

---

[694] Ibid.

[695] Ibid.

[696] Ibid.

[697] Oyeniyi, Lawrence Damilare, Chinonye Esther Ugochukwu, and Noluthando Zamanjomane Mhlongo. "Implementing AI in Banking Customer Service: A Review of Current Trends and Future Applications." *International Journal of Science and Research Archive* 11, no. 2 (April 13, 2024): p. 1493. https://doi.org/10.30574/ijsra.2024.11.2.0639.

[698] Ibid.

[699] Ibid.

[700] Ibid.

[701] Ibid.

[702] Ibid.

[703] Ibid.

[704] Ibid.

[705] Ibid.

[706] Ibid.

[707] Ibid.

[708] Ibid.

[709] Ibid., p. 1494

banking demonstrates adaptation to technological changes and a commitment to satisfying client expectations in the digital age.[710] AI technology has the possibility to modify the banking experience for both individuals and businesses, making strategic development and implementation crucial for the future.[711]

O'Brien and Downie (2024) AI in insurance refers to the automation, and additional technological advances to improve insurance protection and customer service.[712] The insurance sector, including similar banking companies, rely heavily on data.[713] This information assists carriers in determining which insurance policies to offer to specific individuals and what rates to charge.[714] AI can help suppliers enhance their decision-making capabilities, resulting in better customer care and higher profits.[715] The insurance industry has long relied heavily on data and algorithms, such as calculating insurance rates and handling both private and public information throughout the underwriting procedure to evaluate dangers and determine the cost insurance services.[716] However, AI improves those abilities at a much faster and larger scale.[717] The increasing number of insurtech firms using modern technology to assist clients allows them to either give solutions for traditional providers or undergo business competition.[718] AI-powered technology can benefit enterprises that provide insurance to both individual customers and businesses.[719] As a result, insurance companies as well as additional entities in the financial services industry ought to think about starting many AI-powered projects to reap the advantages of this innovative technology.[720]

According to Rao, Badalamenti, and Wilinski (2024), as AI gains popularity, it becomes clear that it is here to stay.[721] Consumers and businesses alike benefit from this connectivity.[722] However, AI, like other new technologies, is not without problems.[723] There are, however, certain flaws and

---

[710] Ibid.

[711] Ibid.

[712] Ibid.

[713] Ibid.

[714] Ibid.

[715] Ibid.

[716] Ibid.

[717] Ibid.

[718] Ibid.

[719] Ibid.

[720] Ibid.

[721] Rao, Nastasha L, Nicholas T Badalamenti, and Nicole E Wilinski. "Artificial Intelligence and the Insurance Industry." State Bar of Michigan, December 2024. https://www.michbar.org/journal/Details/Artificial-intelligence-and-the-insurance-industry?ArticleID=4986.

[722] Ibid.

[723] Ibid.

potential drawbacks to its use.[724] For anybody in or near the insurance sector, the moment to understand AI's abilities — and restrictions — is now.[725] AI's entry into the insurance industry has already resulted in lawsuits.[726] In 2022, collective action was launched against State Farm in the Northern District of Illinois.[727] The complaint claimed that by utilizing AI in claims processing and fraud detection, State Farm discriminated against African American policyholders in violation of the Fair Housing Act.[728] For context, State Farm is accused of collecting data on policyholders, including sex, race, gender, and education.[729] State Farm used this data to develop profiles for its policyholders based on their preferences, attributes, psychological patterns, and IQ.[730] These profiles were then utilized to handle claims.[731] Initial claims were automated using AI, which employs predictive modeling or rules-based decision making to determine whether to settle claims right away or to initiate additional investigation.[732] The AI program learns from the data and evaluates how previous claims were handled before making recommendations for addressing new claims.[733] However, according to the lawsuit, this approach resulted in Black claimants being scrutinized more than white claimants.[734] Finally, it was claimed that State Farm violated 42 U.S. Code § 3604(b) of the Fair Housing Act (FHA), which forbids racial discrimination in services associated with the sale of a home.[735] The court concluded that since certain mortgage brokers compel applicants to acquire homeowners' protection, providing insurance for homeowners constitutes an obligation associated with the selling of a home.[736] It is an example of unanticipated problems caused by AI use.[737]

According to Kumar, Srivastava, and Bisht (2019), the insurance industry has historically had low client involvement.[738] Insurers have the lowest consumer interaction rate compared to other

---

[724] Ibid.
[725] Ibid.
[726] Ibid.
[727] Ibid.
[728] Ibid.
[729] Ibid.
[730] Ibid.
[731] Ibid.
[732] Ibid.
[733] Ibid.
[734] Ibid.
[735] Ibid.
[736] Ibid.
[737] Ibid.
[738] Kumar, Naman, Jayant Dev Srivastava, and Harshit Bisht. "Artificial Intelligence in Insurance Sector." *Journal of the Gujarat Research Society* 21, no. 7 (November 2019): p. 79.

industries.[739] Insurers often have limited connection with end-consumers due to their reliance on intermediaries.[740] For example, brokers receive $45 billion in annual remuneration from insurers globally.[741] Furthermore, the industry's delayed digitization limits insurers' ability to understand customer demands and create solutions.[742]The industry's major difficulties are divided into six verticals: opportunity cost, proper counsel, time consuming, cost, frauds, and bulky processes.[743] These six verticals can be taken up and addressed effectively with technology.[744] Cognitive technologies are rapidly transforming the insurance industry.[745]

In 2017, AI demonstrated its effectiveness in establishing automated settings for increased productivity across multiple business verticals.[746] Insurance businesses can benefit greatly from investing in AI technology that automates executive-level work and improves service quality by assisting agents in making sound decisions.[747] AI is gaining popularity as data becomes more prevalent in professional, personal, and public settings.[748] Digitalization has led to increased data collection from various sources, including corporations, governments, homes, and individuals.[749] Every day, around 2.5 million terabytes of data are created.[750]

Zarifis, Holland, and Milne (2023) business models encompass an organization, its activities, and how it collects and generates revenue.[751] Although the spotlight is on the company itself, a business model may incorporate the organization's partners.[752] One key variation between insurers is whether they try to protect all of the consumer's insurance necessities and operate as a 'one-stop shop' or if they specialize solely on a particular insurance form.[753] A further contrast is the difference amongst entrusted, conventional carriers and emerging competitors.[754] Incumbent

---

[739] Ibid.
[740] Ibid.
[741] Ibid.
[742] Ibid.
[743] Ibid.
[744] Ibid.
[745] Ibid.
[746] Ibid., p. 80
[747] Ibid.
[748] Ibid.
[749] Ibid.
[750] Ibid.
[751] Zarifis, Alex, Christopher P. Holland, and Alistair Milne. "Evaluating the Impact of AI on Insurance: The Four Emerging AI- and Data-Driven Business Models." *Emerald Open Research* 1, no. 1 (October 1, 2019): p. 4. https://doi.org/10.1108/eor-01-2023-0001.

[752] Ibid.
[753] Ibid.
[754] Ibid.

carriers frequently provide various offerings, but newcomers frequently specialize in one product or service, such as automobile coverage.[755]

Hayes (2025) claims that AI has become an adverse factor in managing finances.[756] Today's investors can use strong AI-powered technologies to evaluate massive volumes of economic and other information, detect trends, and come to smarter investing choices.[757] Approximately 90% of investment managers are already utilizing or intend to employ AI in their financial procedures, including 54% currently incorporating AI in multiple manners within their plans.[758] These AI machines go further than mere robotics, using complex ML methods to acquire knowledge on marketplace data instantaneously, and adapting its methods as circumstances fluctuate and fresh knowledge becomes available.[759] While AI does not ensure financial achievement, but offers an entirely novel array of strong instruments, when utilized appropriately, may improve the way humans make decisions and possible financial results.[760]

In the information acquisition stage, AI systems may handle information that is structured (the cost actions, trade volume, bank records) and raw information (media documents, social media emotions, aerial images), concurrently.[761] The amount of information available is impressive—modern platforms such as IBM Watson's accounting software could examine numerous publicly traded organizations in immediate fashion, analyzing over one million points of information every day.[762] This frequently involves innovative sources of data which experienced study groups are unable to observe, like data collected by IoT sensors from towns and factories, patent request linguistic structures, and immediate freight vessel GPS tracking information.[763]

The pattern recognition layer is where AI distinguishes oneself beyond the human eye and conventional algorithms.[764] AI platforms might detect minor associations that standard

---

[755] Ibid.

[756] Hayes, Adam. "7 Unexpected Ways AI Can Transform Your Investment Strategy." Investopedia, January 27, 2025. https://www.investopedia.com/using-ai-to-transform-investment-strategy-8778945#:~:text=Artificial%20intelligence%20(AI)%20has%20emerged,make%20more%20informed%20investment%20decisions.

[757] Ibid.
[758] Ibid.
[759] Ibid.
[760] Ibid.
[761] Ibid.
[762] Ibid.
[763] Ibid.
[764] Ibid.

mathematical approaches might overlook by employing techniques such as quantum machine learning (QML) for sophisticated probability computations and image recognition for analyzing visual information (ranging from graphical representations to aerial images).[765] For example, some systems now use NLP to monitor the psychological aspects of profit call reports instantaneously, while others use large language models (LLMs) to examine and interpret massive amounts of social networking information.[766]

There is a hypothetical application in silicon research.[767] Conventional researchers might concentrate on accounting documents which show stated stock levels and profit margins, but frequently high trading systems monitor price momentum and order movement in real time.[768] An AI system, on the other hand, would take a more sophisticated approach, combining them with various weak indicators to provide insightful data.[769] It may be noticed that an organization's electricity usage has risen slightly over seasonal norms (based on electric company records), whereas their vendors employment advertisements for inspection roles rose heavily (based on job websites and job market information), and research articles with attribution to their exclusive equipment have increased at physics events (based on peer-reviewed databases like ArXiv and Google Scholar).[770]

Ferreria, Gandomi, and Cardoso (2021) state that with the debut of finance computational methods in the 1990s, there has been a lot of research into using AI to invest in stocks.[771] Applying mathematical methods for automating the purchasing procedure offers advantages such as eliminating impulsive choices, discovering and studying trends, and current data usage.[772] This field is currently referred to as Computational Finance.[773] In computational finance, AI approaches are increasingly being used and researched for financial investment.[774] While computers automate most hedge fund trades, 90% still rely on hardcoded procedures.[775] AI has significant potential for

---

[765] Ibid.

[766] Ibid.

[767] Ibid.

[768] Ibid.

[769] Ibid.

[770] Ibid.

[771] Ferreira, Fernando G.D.C., Amir H. Gandomi, and Rodrigo T.N. Cardoso. "Artificial Intelligence Applied to Stock Market Trading: A Review." *IEEE Access* 9 (February 26, 2021): p. 30898. https://doi.org/10.1109/access.2021.3058133.

[772] Ibid.

[773] Ibid.

[774] Ibid.

[775] Ibid.

further improvement, as its applications grow.[776] AI is used in finance for three purposes: optimizing portfolios, forecasting future asset prices, and analyzing sentiment in news and social media.[777] Some works propose combining methodologies from many domains, notwithstanding their unique characteristics.[778] Other computational finance research topics include dynamic system control used within the financial sector, client analysis of behavior, analysis of networks, and financial asset grouping.[779] The calibrated volatility of options is related to futures price changes in the Taiwan stock market.[780] The study found a correlation of around -0.9, indicating that volatility in options can predict futures prices.[781]

Pereira (2025) claims that human intuition, basic understanding, and technical indicators have historically led the stock market.[782] However, AI is changing this paradigm by providing superior algorithms capable of processing enormous amounts of immediately available information roughly just a percentage of the period required by an experienced researcher.[783] AI can produce more accurate predictions than traditional techniques by analyzing complicated trends in market prices, accounting records, indicators of economy, and even headlines in the news.[784]

According to Straut (2024), AI market screeners may be utilized to discover fresh investments depending on the parameters specified by the user, the screener's model, and the sets of data used.[785] Stock screeners may assist investors find the best stocks for trading or spot market trends.[786] These screeners can assist investors in quickly analyzing and acting on possibilities.[787] AI can help analyze and oversee possible risk in investments by evaluating information to uncover or forecast volatility, risks, and possibilities.[788] Instantaneous AI predictions on current affairs, business

---

[776] Ibid.

[777] Ibid.

[778] Ibid.

[779] Ibid.

[780] Ibid.

[781] Ibid.

[782] Pereira, Lester. "The Disruption of AI in Stock Markets: A New Era of Investment Decisions and Automation." Forbes, March 6, 2025. https://www.forbes.com/councils/forbestechcouncil/2025/03/06/the-disruption-of-ai-in-stock-markets-a-new-era-of-investment-decisions-and-automation/.

[783] Ibid.

[784] Ibid.

[785] Straut, Nicolas. "How to Use AI to Make Money with Investing." Forbes, July 25, 2024. https://www.forbes.com/sites/investor-hub/article/how-to-use-ai-to-make-money-investing/.

[786] Ibid.

[787] Ibid.

[788] Ibid.

headlines, and financial variables could assist a consumer in changing his or her portfolio by immediately unloading risky holdings.[789] AI-powered assessment of risks can assist in enhancing the consumer's portfolio results in an efficient and timely manner, while also lowering expenses through automated evaluation.[790]

Robo-advisors are automated investment systems that rebalance portfolios and capture tax losses.[791] They are frequently tailored to the investor's age, time horizon, and aspirations.[792] Algorithmic trading use AI to execute trades based on user-defined circumstances and data.[793] These techniques can work together if a trader uses a robo-advisor with an additional safe approach and automated trading with a lower percentage of their investment account to execute dangerous, high-return bets.[794]

AI can help in managing a portfolio by proposing or implementing adjustments that preserve the proper allocation of assets, growth, and restoring equilibrium according to the prospect for rewards or to prevent volatility.[795] Managing a portfolio may be expensive because of the requirement for human evaluation, but AI offers the ability to automate repetitive jobs while maintaining or surpassing individual effectiveness.[796] AI can provide insights that assist investors in making decisions by processing huge amounts of data, including market data, financial reports, and news.[797] AI assists investors in discovering new opportunities and making smarter investment selections by recognizing patterns and analyzing trends.[798] Using AI to analyze data allows investors to act more swiftly and efficiently.[799] AI can be used to evaluate investor sentiment toward certain companies, such as small-cap value stocks, or markets, assisting individuals in identifying possibilities or possible modifications to their holdings.[800] AI does this by analyzing language and emotion in information sources such as social networking sites or publications to forecast stock, industry, or price movements.[801]

---

[789] Ibid.
[790] Ibid.
[791] Ibid.
[792] Ibid.
[793] Ibid.
[794] Ibid.
[795] Ibid.
[796] Ibid.
[797] Ibid.
[798] Ibid.
[799] Ibid.
[800] Ibid.
[801] Ibid.

Chua, Pal, and Banerjee (2023) emphasize the importance of trustworthiness as well as apparent precision in stock-market investments.[802] Ultimately, whenever AI is designed to generate forecasts, users' decision to embrace machine-generated guidance may be heavily influenced by their trust in AI and perception of its accuracy.[803] The secretive characteristics of investment-related AI machines may increase the need for trust and perceived accuracy.[804] Given the stock market's volatility, investors may have regret aversion, defined as the dread of making a terrible selection.[805] This may end up in inaction or a deliberate attempt to prevent self-blame.[806] AI-generated investment recommendations may lead to increased vigilance in decision-making, leading investors to either reject them or trust the technology.[807]

Rasouli, Chiruvolu, and Risheh (2023) suggest that in today's competitive investment scene, funds prioritize efficient transaction sourcing and improved insights.[808] While funds are already devoting large resources to these two jobs, they cannot be scaled using traditional ways, hence there is a rise in automation.[809] Many third-party software providers have lately emerged to fulfill this demand with productivity solutions, however often fail owing to a lack of personalization for funding, privacy concerns, and the inherent limitations of software use scenarios.[810] As a result, many major and smaller funds are establishing their own AI systems, which is transforming the sector.[811] These tools become smarter through direct interactions with the fund, enabling individualized use cases.[812] New advances in big computational models of languages, such as ChatGPT, have opened up opportunities for other funds to create their own AI systems.[813] In two years, not having an AI platform will become a competitive disadvantage.[814] Funds demand a practical plan and risk assessment for AI platforms.[815]

---

[802] Chua, Alton Y.K., Anjan Pal, and Snehasish Banerjee. "Ai-Enabled Investment Advice: Will Users Buy It?" *Computers in Human Behavior* 138 (2023): 107481. https://doi.org/10.1016/j.chb.2022.107481.

[803] Ibid.
[804] Ibid.
[805] Ibid.
[806] Ibid.
[807] Ibid.
[808] Rasouli, Mohammad, Ravi Chiruvolu, and Ali Risheh. "AI for Investment: A Platform Disruption." *arXiv preprint arXiv:2311.06251* (2023).
[809] Ibid.
[810] Ibid.
[811] Ibid.
[812] Ibid.
[813] Ibid.
[814] Ibid.
[815] Ibid.

According to Bi, et al. (2024), as AI technology advances, employing ML to predict market patterns may become more feasible.[816] AI has been a popular research topic in academia, with applications ranging from image identification to NLP and quantitative investment.[817] Quantitative investment is popular among financial institutions and investors because it provides predictable profits via analyzing information, building models and program trading.[818] AI-based statistical investing strategies are emerging as a significant application in the area of quantitative investment.[819] The traditional quantitative investment strategy utilizes computers to identify possible price and intrinsic value laws using economic timing information.[820] This approach blends academic expertise with practical expertise to achieve consistent returns.[821] Quantitative investment relies on extensive economic information as well as a successful conceptual framework.[822] Advancements in data mining technology enable more precise investment decisions and instantaneous trading, leading to improved accuracy and timeliness in securities trading.[823] For more than a decade, China has been seeing an increase in quantitative investment.[824] Investment institutions are increasingly adopting AI technologies.[825] After three rounds of rapid iteration and improvement, AI technology is now being used to support quantitative investment in the new air outlet.[826] Investors worldwide are anxious about inflation in the US and the Federal Reserve's decision to halt increasing interest rates.[827] This has an impact on international assets, particularly the Chinese stock market.[828] AI technology can significantly enhance quantitative investment strategy research.[829]

According to Krause (2025), several software equities underperformed in 2025, particularly after President Donald Trump's tariff-based trade policy raised concerns about a potential U.S.

[816] Bi, Shuochen, Wenqing Bao, Jue Xiao, Jiangshan Wang, and Tingting Deng. "Application and Practice of AI Technology in Quantitative Investment." *Information Systems and Economics* 5, no. 2 (2024): p. 124. https://doi.org/10.23977/infse.2024.050217.

[817] Ibid.
[818] Ibid.
[819] Ibid.
[820] Ibid., p. 124-125
[821] Ibid., p. 125
[822] Ibid.
[823] Ibid.
[824] Ibid.
[825] Ibid.
[826] Ibid.
[827] Ibid.
[828] Ibid.
[829] Ibid.

recession.[830] Investors should pay special attention to the heated rivalry in AI models.[831] Competition between US and open-source AI models like DeepSeek and others might flare up in the event of a US-China trade war.[832]

According to Chauhan (2025), investors were trading down AI shares and taking gains in order to safeguard their wealth in the face of continuous turbulence and financial instability induced by Trump's initiatives to manipulate the market in his favor.[833] The tech-heavy Nasdaq Composite index is officially in bear market territory, and it is unclear whether the downturn will persist given the current trade dispute sparked by Trump's tariff measures.[834] JPMorgan analysts estimate that tariffs will cause the US economy to enter a recession in 2025.[835] So, it is hardly surprising that investors are keeping on the deterrent and preserving their wealth.[836] Around the same period of time, astute traders with excess capital might want to think about buying stocks of leading AI companies that continue to trade at reasonable values despite the current sell-off.[837] AI adoption is still in its infancy, but its application is predicted to develop significantly due to the productivity advantages that it may give.[838]

Price forecasting, according to Abdollahi and Mahmoudi (2021), is an important aspect of making economic decisions.[839] Forecasts are used for various purposes, including speculative income, government policy optimization, and business decision-making.[840] The price of gold, like all other goods, is determined by supply and demand.[841] Traders have been paying careful consideration to the fluctuating gold market in recent years, citing the possibility of significant profits in the near future.[842] Gold is the sole metal that has retained its intrinsic worth throughout

---

[830] Krause, Reinhardt. "AI Stocks Face 'show Me' Moment. Trump Tariffs Loom over AI Models, Software." Investor's Business Daily, April 14, 2025. https://www.investors.com/news/technology/artificial-intelligence-stocks/.

[831] Ibid.
[832] Ibid.
[833] Chauhan, Harsh. "2 No-Brainer Artificial Intelligence (AI) Stocks to Buy Right Now." Yahoo! Finance, April 9, 2025. https://finance.yahoo.com/news/2-no-brainer-artificial-intelligence-075500020.html.

[834] Ibid.
[835] Ibid.
[836] Ibid.
[837] Ibid.
[838] Ibid.
[839] Abdollahi, Jafar, and Laya Mahmoudi. "Investigation of artificial intelligence in stock market prediction studies." In *10th International Conference on Innovation and Research in Engineering Science*. 2021.
[840] Ibid.
[841] Ibid.
[842] Ibid.

the recessions and banking crises.[843] Additionally, gold prices are tightly linked to different products.[844] The longer-term gold price projection serves as a warning system for investors in the event of unforeseen market dangers.[845] Gold prices are influenced by future supply and demand, unlike long-term investments like equities or bonds.[846] The gold price is forecasted based on the market's perception of its value, which is influenced by various factors such as inflation, currency fluctuations, and political unrest.[847]

Rahmani, et al. (2023) argue that AI has the ability to automate the workforce.[848] Technology cuts payroll expenses and enhances efficiency by employing more skilled employees.[849] The rise in inflation has been a major worldwide problem lately.[850] The median per capita income has never risen to date.[851] Individuals continue to pay taxes, bills, and purchase homes.[852] In these conditions, individuals are more prone to spend than they earn.[853] Precisely, consumers are going to explore strategies to increase their investment assets.[854] Traders with experience are using ML to anticipate stock values.[855] Each product has distinct characteristics, including market liquidity and size.[856] Modifying feature selection or data modeling could help solve this issue.[857] AI now helps investors make rapid and precise decisions.[858] Investors are skeptical about AI-based trading algorithms due of their uncertainty.[859] To lessen risks, merging multiple algorithms aims to increase investor trust.[860] Currently, there exist multiple ML models.[861] Two algorithms stand out: Long Short-Term Memory (LSTM) and Auto-Regressive Integrated Moving Average (ARIMA).[862] Collaboration

---

[843] Ibid.

[844] Ibid.

[845] Ibid.

[846] Ibid.

[847] Ibid.

[848] Rahmani, Amir Masoud, Bahareh Rezazadeh, Majid Haghparast, Wei-Che Chang, and Shen Guan Ting. "Applications of Artificial Intelligence in the Economy, Including Applications in Stock Trading, Market Analysis, and Risk Management." *IEEE Access* 11 (2023): p. 80770. https://doi.org/10.1109/access.2023.3300036.

[849] Ibid.

[850] Ibid.

[851] Ibid.

[852] Ibid.

[853] Ibid.

[854] Ibid.

[855] Ibid.

[856] Ibid.

[857] Ibid.

[858] Ibid.

[859] Ibid.

[860] Ibid.

[861] Ibid.

[862] Ibid.

between these two algorithms can create a more trustworthy and sustainable model.[863]

Chopra and Sharma (2021) state that predicting a stock market's future price movement if difficult because of the irregularity and volatility in the data.[864] The unpredictable and complex nature of the stock market has made it challenging for investors to make timely investing decisions.[865] When calculating prices for stocks, two traditional hypotheses need to be examined: the random walk (RW) theory and the efficient market hypothesis (EMH).[866] As stated by EMH, an asset's value absorbs any available trading information at one time.[867] Price swings are unpredictable because market participants seek the greatest utilization of any known expertise, and novel data arrives at random.[868] According to the RW theory, stock prices follow no trends or patterns, resulting in spontaneous deviations from prior prices.[869] This means that investors cannot foresee the market.[870] A different approach that opposes EMH is Paul Samuelson's martingale model, claiming based on every available detail, present costs are most accurate forecasts of an event's fate.[871] The most recent observed value is the most reliable predictor of the final outcome.[872]

The veracity of the EMH and RW theories has been disputed.[873] With the rise of computational and smart finance, as well as behavioral finance, economists have proposed the inefficient market hypothesis (IMH).[874] This theory suggests that market mechanisms are not always effective.[875] Psychology, transaction costs, information asymmetry, and emotions are all elements that contribute to market inefficiencies.[876] Many studies have employed AI to support their views, however the fact that some players continuously exceed the market advises that the EMH may not be completely factual.[877] The fractal market hypothesis (FMH) is a feasible alternative to the

---

[863] Ibid.
[864] Chopra, Ritika, and Gagan Deep Sharma. "Application of Artificial Intelligence in Stock Market Forecasting: A Critique, Review, and Research Agenda." *Journal of Risk and Financial Management* 14, no. 11 (November 4, 2021): 526. https://doi.org/10.3390/jrfm14110526.

[865] Ibid.
[866] Ibid.
[867] Ibid.
[868] Ibid.
[869] Ibid.
[870] Ibid.
[871] Ibid.
[872] Ibid.
[873] Ibid.
[874] Ibid.
[875] Ibid.
[876] Ibid.
[877] Ibid.

EMH.[878] The FMH views market stability as matching investor investment horizons, while the EMH assumes equilibrium.[879]

FMH investigates the stock market's everyday unpredictability as well as the volatility encountered throughout crises and crashes, and it offers a plausible rationale for investor conduct throughout the market cycle, covering periods of prosperity and despair.[880] Interestingly, it takes into account irregular correlations in series challenges, resulting in a helpful hypothesis for forecasting stocks along with additional series challenges or financial market problems.[881] Today, the usefulness and advantages of prediction in decision- and policymaking are widely acknowledged over several proportions.[882] Techniques with less predicting errors are more likely to survive and perform well.[883] Numerous people, especially academia, financial professionals, and traders or investors, are looking for a better technique that would yield high returns.[884]

Market price forecasting is based on historical data of important factors and habits improves prediction efficiency.[885] To accurately predict, external phenomena such as recessions or expansions, in addition to high- or low-volatility phases effected by cyclical and other short-term swings in whole demand, must be considered.[886] One of the most important criteria for everyone working in a financial environment is their capacity to accurately forecast fluctuations in market prices while making sound judgments according to those forecasts.[887] Stock market predictions have served as a subject of study for a number of decades.[888] The monetary gain could be regarded the most important aspect of stock-market forecasting.[889] A system that consistently identifies the losers and winners in a highly competitive situation makes additional revenue for its owner.[890]

---

[878] Ibid.
[879] Ibid.
[880] Ibid.
[881] Ibid.
[882] Ibid.
[883] Ibid.
[884] Ibid.
[885] Ibid.
[886] Ibid.
[887] Ibid.
[888] Ibid.
[889] Ibid.
[890] Ibid.

5 AI AND FOOD SERVICE

Each time I visit a fast-food joint, there are ordering kiosks where customers would order their meals without contact with an employee. The cons of fast-food kiosks are that they do not accept cash. The first thing that I had in my mind is that entry-level fast-food workers in several states were demanding a raise to $15/hour although basic training would be provided on the job. There are posts on social media of bad food and rude customer service versus $15/hour wage. Fast food chains had to compensate for the wage increases by installing kiosks. Secondly, many chains do not want to hire many employees and would encourage customers to use the kiosks instead.

According to Gibbs (2022), McDonald's had begun testing its first robot restaurant in Fort Worth, Texas, which sparked both discussion and intrigue.[891] The branch is completely automated, requiring no human interaction to order and pick up his or her favorite food on a conveyor belt.[892] The introvert's dream went viral after TikTok and Instagram user foodiemunster posted a video from inside.[893] The film, which has received 1.2 million views, demonstrates how clients may order fast food using computerized screens and pick it via a machine.[894] The restaurant is the latest addition to McDonald's "Accelerating the Arches" growth strategy, which prioritizes creativity to improve customer relations.[895]

---

[891] Gibbs, Alice. "Welcome to the First Ever McDonald's Where You're Served by Robots-in Texas." Newsweek, December 24, 2022. https://www.newsweek.com/first-ever-mcdonalds-served-robots-texas-1769116.

[892] Ibid.
[893] Ibid.
[894] Ibid.
[895] Ibid.

According to Gerken (2024), McDonald's pulled AI-powered ordering equipment out of its drive-thru outlets in the United States after consumers posted amusing errors online.[896] In 2019, IBM launched a testing of the system, which processes orders with voice recognition software.[897] It has not, however, been completely dependable, leading to internet sensations of weird, misread orders that include bacon-topped ice cream to several hundred dollars' worth of Chicken McNuggets.[898] The technology has been contentious from the start, with initial fears focused on its capacity to render workers redundant.[899] It nevertheless is increasingly clear that eliminating real staff members in restaurants could not be as simple as consumers originally feared—or the program's supporters anticipated.[900]

According to Stoffers (2024), automated kiosks had unintentionally raised the burden on the kitchen staff by generating larger and more tailored orders, especially during peak hours, in comparison with conventional point of sale purchases.[901] It implies that complicated and bigger requests arrive in the kitchen, frequently everything simultaneously during peak times.[902] Customers are frequently persuaded to spend more than they would if ordering face-to-face, thanks to images that highlight add-ons and upgrades.[903] With additional appetizers to sweets recommendations, kiosks gently push bigger purchases, hence raising the standard bill amount.[904]

According to Shahota (2024), the incorporation of AI into the restaurant business is transforming eating experiences and operational efficiencies.[905] By streamlining cooking operations to customizing interactions with consumers, AI is improving each element of the food service industry.[906] AI has already been applied into restaurants, dramatically improving customer service.[907]

---

[896] Gerken, Tom. "McDonalds Removes AI Drive-Throughs after Order Errors." BBC News, June 18, 2024. https://www.bbc.com/news/articles/c722gne7qngo.

[897] Ibid.
[898] Ibid.
[899] Ibid.
[900] Ibid.
[901] Stoffers, Carl. "The Unintended Consequences of Fast-Food Ordering Kiosks." Entrepreneur, September 27, 2024. https://www.entrepreneur.com/franchises/the-unintended-consequences-of-fast-food-ordering-kiosks/480269.

[902] Ibid.
[903] Ibid.
[904] Ibid.
[905] Sahota, Neil. "AI in the Culinary World: Revolutionizing Restaurant Ops & Customer Experience." Forbes, March 13, 2024. https://www.forbes.com/sites/neilsahota/2024/03/13/ai-in-the-culinary-world-revolutionizing-restaurant-ops--customer-experience/.

[906] Ibid.
[907] Ibid.

Chatbots, for example, are increasingly being used to book bookings and answer client questions.[908] McDonald's bought Apprente, an AI business, with the goal of integrating voice-based AI systems into its drive-thru kiosks, allowing for quicker and more precise ordering.[909] In a comparable manner Domino's Pizza employs Dom, an AI aid, for orders online, a move that simplified the procedure and increased consumer retention.[910] Exceeding customer service, AI can help personalize eating experiences.[911] Restaurants utilize AI technologies to analyze client data and provide personalized recommendations and promotions.[912] Starbucks' Deep Brew program is a significant example, as it offers customers personalized recommendations based on their previous purchases and tastes.[913]

AI is drastically altering the fast-food sector, increasing productivity and defining consumer interactions.[914] Over the last 10 years, AI-powered kiosks, electronic menus, drive-thru robotics, and delivery advances became the norm, while big chains spending considerably in next-gen innovation.[915] Wendy's intends to extend its FreshAI drive-thru system to 600 sites, utilizing voice identification to simplify requests.[916] The parent company of Kentucky Fried Chicken (KFC), Pizza Hut, and Taco Bell; Yum! Brands, introduced 'Byte by Yum!,' an AI-generated software platform that enhances ordering via the internet, cooking management, and delivery operation.[917] As establishments adopt to AI-powered processes, delivery service providers are following suit.[918] Uber Eats utilizes AI to maximize routes, anticipate times of delivery, and customize suggestions, whereas Serve Robotics' automated curbside robots are currently delivering meals for the Uber Eats platform.[919] Besides contributing to fast food, AI-powered robots are having an impact on coffee services and food distribution.[920] The Second Cup Coffee Company has introduced Mozo, a robo-barista, in Beirut to improve café productivity and uniformity.[921] Additionally, the Chulchul Box, a robo-chef vending machine, serves hot exquisite meals in under 90 seconds, meeting the need for

---

[908] Ibid.
[909] Ibid.
[910] Ibid.
[911] Ibid.
[912] Ibid.
[913] Ibid.
[914] Ibid.
[915] Ibid.
[916] Ibid.
[917] Ibid.
[918] Ibid.
[919] Ibid.
[920] Ibid.
[921] Ibid.

rapid service and excellent food in metropolitan cuisine.[922]

AI optimizes kitchen tasks and the preparation of food.[923] Zume Pizza, for example, employs AI-powered robots to help in pizza preparation, increasing productivity and consistency.[924] The aforementioned machines can evenly distribute marinara sauce and check the cooking process, improving pizza consistency.[925] According to Council (2023), Zume Pizza ceased business and liquidated its assets because the cheese kept slipping off in the making process when the truck hit on potholes and speed humps.[926]

Furthermore, stock oversight is a field in which AI has achieved great progress.[927] AI algorithms forecast supply demands according to past information and prospective bookings, assisting establishments in avoiding overproduction or deficits.[928] Dishoom, a London-based food company, introduced an AI application for stock control, which decreased wasted food by 20%.[929]

AI is transforming the creation of menus by studying consumer tastes and current market conditions.[930] Computer programs recommend modifications to the menu which are expected to be appealing to consumers, hence increasing profits.[931] In one instance, an eatery serving sushi in Japan used AI to adapt their offerings depending on client input, resulting in a 10% improvement in consumer happiness.[932] In the field of culinary architecture, AI assists culinary professionals develop unique dishes. IBM's Chef Watson, an AI technology, helps cooks create unique meals by recommending combinations of ingredients that ordinary culinary professionals might fail to consider.[933] Such creativity led to in the development of distinctive and well-known dishes in a

---

[922] Ibid.

[923] Ibid.

[924] Ibid.

[925] Ibid.

[926] Council, Stephen. "Bay Area-Founded Pizza Startup Zume Reportedly Shuts down after Raising $445 Million." SF Gate, June 5, 2023. https://www.sfgate.com/tech/article/zume-pizza-startup-shuts-down-18136126.php.

[927] Ibid.

[928] Ibid.

[929] Ibid.

[930] Ibid.

[931] Ibid.

[932] Ibid.

[933] Ibid.

number of upscale eateries, such the chocolate Austrian burrito and the Vietnamese apple kebob.[934]

Marketing is another area where AI is proving to be extremely useful in the eating industry.[935] AI algorithms use client information to generate tailored advertising strategies.[936] As an instance, Chili's, an eatery chain in the United States, employs AI to evaluate consumer information and create targeted advertisements, resulting in more consumer involvement and revenue.[937] improving their menu selections.[938] AI systems evaluate critiques and feedback from several sources to deliver relevant information.[939] TGI Friday's introduced an AI-powered advertising system that evaluates client tastes and input, resulting in a considerable improvement in marketing strategy and customer experience.[940]

Going forward, AI holds the potential to significantly disrupt the restaurant industry.[941] AR and VR are paving the road for interactive eating: Dining establishments will leverage AI and VR/AR to offer interactive eating encounters, like digital vineyard excursions for sampling wines or themed eating activities.[942] There is also the AI-powered individual diet helper.[943] Imagine an AI algorithm which examines all a person eats and potentially consume.[944] The personalized nutritional advisors could prove extremely beneficial for assisting individuals control their food intake and general wellbeing by recommending food options according to specific wellness objectives as well as food limitations.[945] The equipment will then be used to provide autonomous quality assurance.[946] Eateries will use AI to maintain constant checks on quality in the preparation area, guaranteeing every single dish meets expectations.[947] Furthermore, in an additional conventional application, restaurants might employ AI for advanced analytics and predictive modeling of trends.[948] AI algorithms are going to be successful at forecasting future cuisine patterns, allowing eateries to remain far ahead of the game with food innovation.[949] Lastly, the food environment will be built on

---

[934] Ibid.
[935] Ibid.
[936] Ibid.
[937] Ibid.
[938] Ibid.
[939] Ibid.
[940] Ibid.
[941] Ibid.
[942] Ibid.
[943] Ibid.
[944] Ibid.
[945] Ibid.
[946] Ibid.
[947] Ibid.
[948] Ibid.
[949] Ibid.

the foundation of AI-powered mealtime.[950] Upcoming eateries may have AI-powered robots that assist in serving food as well as preparing with chefs, creating a one-of-a-kind dining experience.[951]

AI integration in the restaurant sector is more than a fad; it is a revolutionary movement that is reshaping eating experiences and operational efficiencies.[952] AI has the potential to improve customer service and revolutionize kitchen operations.[953] As technology progresses, the opportunity for AI in eateries grows exponentially, offering not solely increased productivity and client fulfillment, as well as novel eating encounters.[954] Adopting AI is critical to eateries looking to remain viable and provide outstanding customer service within a fast growing business.[955]

There are robots trained to be servers in restaurants. According to Dickinson (2023), an owner cannot run a restaurant without workers.[956] And, as labor shortages persist across the industry, operators are increasingly turning to digital solutions to assist solve the problem.[957] The robotic waiter, or robo-waiter, is among the more innovative, front-facing options that are presently popular in the casual, full-service sector.[958] These fully automated robots run food and bus dishware, and they can occasionally even serve as hosts and direct guests to their tables.[959] They have been praised for relieving the stress of understaffed teams and decreasing some of the tedious duties that strain existing servers.[960] Robo-waiters have been around for a while, and as technology progresses, more operators are hopping on board.[961] However, the solution is not necessarily appropriate for everyone.[962]

According to Ewing-Chow (2025), AI tendencies are transforming the meal business, from manufacturing and hygiene to tailored meals and better distribution networks.[963] As businesses

---

[950] Ibid.

[951] Ibid.

[952] Ibid.

[953] Ibid.

[954] Ibid.

[955] Ibid.

[956] Dickinson, Grace. "How Do Robotic Waiters Work & Are They Right for Your Restaurant?" Back of House, February 21, 2023. https://backofhouse.io/resources/how-do-robotic-waiters-work-and-are-they-right-for-your-restaurant.

[957] Ibid.

[958] Ibid.

[959] Ibid.

[960] Ibid.

[961] Ibid.

[962] Ibid.

[963] Ewing-Chow, Daphne. "The Latest AI Trends Transforming the Food Industry." Forbes, March 18, 2025. https://www.forbes.com/sites/daphneewingchow/2025/03/18/these-are-the-latest-ai-trends-transforming-the-food-industry/.

address wasted food, security issues, workforce constraints, and shifting consumer needs, the AI-powered foodtech industry is expected to reach $27.73 billion before 2029.[964] The increase is being driven on the demand of personalized dietary habits, tougher hygiene standards, optimization of supply chains, and environmental responsibility, ushering in a modern generation in how the world is fed.[965] With meal creation platforms like KLEVER AI, Ai Palette, and TasteGPT to analysis platforms like Google's Gemini AI, that helps consumers find emerging eateries, AI is transforming the worldwide meal sector in ways that consumers rarely see.[966]

SNAQ, a diabetes platform, has released AI-powered meal glucose prediction, which allows users to foresee their glycemic response before eating a mouthful, as has Spore.bio's ability to detect bacterial numbers in food and drink in seconds, it is no surprise that AI in the food and beverage industry is booming.[967] AI-driven foodtech is expected to increase at a 34.5% per year until 2034, exceeding the total AI market and altering how we eat.[968]

This shift goes past eateries and customer wellness, with big producers of food adopting AI to improve its business operations.[969] Corporations like Danone work with Microsoft to improve operations and optimize manufacturing, while customer-facing solutions like Spoon Guru assist people achieve their dietary goals.[970] Mehta recognizes the Canadian Food Innovation Network (CFIN) on their contribution to promoting AI use throughout this sector, by increasing hygiene and distribution to fine-tuning cost tactics.[971] In the meantime, firms such as Stocky AI utilize AI to transform the way businesses handle inventory and reduce wasteful consumption, highlighting the technology's broad impact on the food industry.[972]

With workforce constraints and frequent volatility within the restaurant business, eateries are turning to AI-powered technology to improve productivity to satisfy consumers' desire for expediency.[973] Robo-chefs are able to weigh ingredients, cook faster, and assure food safety without the need for human participation.[974] Researchers at the University of Tokyo's JSK Robotics

---

[964] Ibid.
[965] Ibid.
[966] Ibid.
[967] Ibid.
[968] Ibid.
[969] Ibid.
[970] Ibid.
[971] Ibid.
[972] Ibid.
[973] Ibid.
[974] Ibid.

Laboratory created an automated system able to fry an egg according to a recipe, whereas Aniai's Alpha Grill, which won the 2023 Kitchen Innovation Award, is capable of making eight burger patties in less than a minute thanks to a dual-sided grill and integrated auto-cleaning characteristics.[975] AI is also revolutionizing household kitchens, with inventions such as Moley Robotics' robo-chef and mobile applications that examine food procurement to provide individualized dietary information.[976] AI is revolutionizing food preparation by making it faster, safer, and more convenient, using ChatGPT-generated recipes and superior robotic cooking equipment.[977]

As new tariffs raise food prices and labor shortages linger, many distributors are looking for ways to decrease costs and increase efficiency.[978] Choco, a firm dedicated to optimizing the supply chain for food products, recently introduced Autopilot, an AI solution which allows suppliers of food to execute requests sans the need for human intervention.[979] Autopilot continuously evaluates requests that come in, verifies the precision, and then simultaneously executes items right away or marks them to be reviewed review.[980] This lowers having employees to laboriously submit requests and allows them to concentrate on other tasks.[981] After introducing Choco AI in 2023, the organization has attempted to improve transaction administration using voicemail, SMS, WhatsApp, and email.[982]

AI is revolutionizing dietary habits, bringing better nutrition easier and economical.[983] Fuddle, an AI-powered food organizer and recipe aid, allows consumers to generate personalized meals according to their eating preferences, allergies, and relevant ingredients.[984] In a similar manner RxDiet, an AI-powered customized diet app, creates customized meal schedules and provides fresh ingredients.[985] In the meantime, Kirin's Flavor-Enhancing Electronic Salt Spoon improves the flavor of low-salt dishes through employing small amounts of electricity to gather sodium ion molecules, urging people to eat less salt.[986]

AI additionally enables companies replicate conventional dishes using more nutritious, more

---

[975] Ibid.
[976] Ibid.
[977] Ibid.
[978] Ibid.
[979] Ibid.
[980] Ibid.
[981] Ibid.
[982] Ibid.
[983] Ibid.
[984] Ibid.
[985] Ibid.
[986] Ibid.

environmentally conscious components by leveraging molecular innovation.[987]   Producers can replicate goods (like cheese) with plant-based or lab-grown ingredients using systems which evaluate taste substances, finding important molecules for flavor, consistency, and melting, resulting in AI-produced copies that are closely identical to the genuine item.[988] Utilizing the concepts, AI-produced food eliminates allergies, reduces environmental impact, and improves dietary profiles while maintaining taste.[989] Deasey Weinstein praises NotCo in Latin America and Climax Foods in North America for developing AI-engineered animal food alternatives that nearly resemble the flavor and texture of conventional dairy and meat.[990]

AI is transforming inspection of food and quality control by increasing contaminant identification, maintaining item uniformity, improving shelf-life forecasts, forecasting risks, and monitoring compliance to improve safety and health for the public.[991] Nestlé's AI-generated optical assessment technologies are revolutionizing standards in the manufacturing of food, while Danone's collaboration with Sight Machine has improved continuous surveillance in dairy facilities.[992] The United Kingdom Health Security Agency (UKHSA) is looking into using AI to identify food-borne epidemics by monitoring web reviews of restaurants seeking references of illnesses such as diarrhea and vomiting, in addition to particular foods.[993] UKHSA scientists evaluated various AI models' capacity to determine and locate significant content in numerous reviews.[994]   Because a lot of intestinal illness goes untreated, AI might lead to a more full understanding of outbreak origins and patterns.[995] In the meantime, Coca-Cola (with a stake in AI business Agnext) is enhancing beverage inspections for quality, while Unilever's takeover of Carver Korea advances AI in aesthetic manufacturing of foods.[996]

AI is helping to lessen the environmental effect of food around the world by reducing food waste and streamlining supply systems.[997] MOA Foodtech, a Spanish AI-driven fermentation firm, converts trash to useful meals, whereas Tomorrow, a Seattle-based business, is revolutionizing the refrigeration sector by utilizing AI to extend produce preservation.[998] AI improves forecasting of

---

[987] Ibid.
[988] Ibid.
[989] Ibid.
[990] Ibid.
[991] Ibid.
[992] Ibid.
[993] Ibid.
[994] Ibid.
[995] Ibid.
[996] Ibid.
[997] Ibid.
[998] Ibid.

demand and operations.[999] Shops such as Coop and Carrefour use Google's AI technologies to reduce wasted food, whereas Unilever uses Google's Tracemark system to increase transparency in the supply chain and prevent degradation.[1000]

Entrepreneurs are cashing on the AI-powered sustainable agriculture movement.[1001] In London, Bright Tide's Sustain.AI Accelerator is fostering an atmosphere of collaboration amongst innovators and corporate managers, whereas EIT Food, an European effort for food sustainability creativity, focuses on AI-powered technologies to assist with making the food industry more environmentally friendly.[1002]

The World Food Programme (WFP) and other United Nations (UN) organizations are using AI to combat hunger.[1003] HungerMap LIVE monitors and forecasts food security in near real time using big data and predictive analytics, whereas GeoTar, which is currently used in Afghanistan, Chad, and Bangladesh, uses drone and satellite data to increase food assistance pointing precision.[1004] WFP's AI Sandbox effort promotes innovation and cooperation by enabling professionals to create and scale AI-driven solutions to food security concerns.[1005] As AI develops to affect food regulations, it may favor corporate-driven cultivation methods instead of more equitable, grassroots ones.[1006] objectives instead of exacerbating current inequality.[1007]

AI is fast changing the way meals are grown, eaten, and enjoyed; yet, its complete influence continues to emerge, clearing the path towards an era of personalized nutrition which customizes menus to specific nutritional requirements.[1008] As AI advances, food is unlikely to be an all-inclusive experience.[1009] AI is ready to propel an industry away from massive production and toward complete nutrition, in which food is no longer merely a calorie source but also a method for improving quality of life.[1010] AI developments in the food industry extend above simply rendering operations more rapid and cheap; are altering how people eat, the way it is produced, and, eventually, why food

---

[999] Ibid.
[1000] Ibid.
[1001] Ibid.
[1002] Ibid.
[1003] Ibid.
[1004] Ibid.
[1005] Ibid.
[1006] Ibid.
[1007] Ibid.
[1008] Ibid.
[1009] Ibid.
[1010] Ibid.

integrates within the larger experience of humans and the world.[1011]

According to Kumar, et al. (2021), AI has certain key benefits in the food industry, such as soil surveillance, robocropping, and forecasting.[1012] In the current situation, the food industry is contemplating the advantages of AI-powered results.[1013] Computerized vision and algorithms for DL are crucial parts of AI-based systems as they study the order of data or knowledge received by AI-based agents to observe soil and crop wellness growth.[1014] Computerized systems offer clients an awareness of their soil's advantages and limitations.[1015] The primary purpose of the developed system is to recognize damaged crops and establish the optimum path for normal growth of crops.[1016]

In the Soil Monitoring (SM) situation, after a farmer submits a sample of farm soil to the surveillance body, the consumer obtains a full summary of the field soil components.[1017] The results indicate appropriate decisions for fungi, bacteria, and microbiological development.[1018] Japan used the first AI-based drone for crop dusting in 1980.[1019] Today, many organizations use agriculture AI and aerial technologies to watch on crop health.[1020] The company's major objective is to cut costs and increase crop growth.[1021] Users must initially pre-program the drone's route prior to merging it with the mobile device.[1022] After that, the computer vision would record certain images for inspection reasons.[1023]

The IoT influences crop and soil management decisions.[1024] SM with IoT is an AI tool that helps farmers and food companies maximize on their economies, reduce disease risks, and optimize the use of existing assets.[1025] Sensors monitor the temperature of the soil, nitrogen, phosphorus, and

---

[1011] Ibid.
[1012] Kumar, Indrajeet, Jyoti Rawat, Noor Mohd, and Shahnawaz Husain. "Opportunities of Artificial Intelligence and Machine Learning in the Food Industry." *Journal of Food Quality* 2021, no. 1 (July 12, 2021): p. 2. https://doi.org/10.1155/2021/4535567.

[1013] Ibid.
[1014] Ibid.
[1015] Ibid.
[1016] Ibid.
[1017] Ibid.
[1018] Ibid.
[1019] Ibid.
[1020] Ibid.
[1021] Ibid.
[1022] Ibid.
[1023] Ibid.
[1024] Ibid.
[1025] Ibid.

potassium (NPK) stages, moisture, oxygen, photosynthetic radiation, and water content levels.[1026] The collected information from the various sensors is then transferred to the data center or the cloud for proper decision-making so that appropriate action may be conducted on time.[1027] Analyzing and visualizing received data can improve resource use.[1028] To optimize crop output and quality, it is important to monitor soil trends and make appropriate decisions based on the circumstances.[1029] Agriculture-based IoT is known as smart agriculture.[1030] The IoT-based food sector is known as the smart food industry.[1031] IoT-based agriculture focuses on soil monitoring, weather forecasting, and crop monitoring.[1032] IoT-based agriculture relies heavily on weather and irrigation systems.[1033] Smart farm elucidations come with an exquisite atmosphere, including high-quality air and a well-maintained watering system.[1034]

As technology advances, the food business adopts current technology-based techniques to increase productivity.[1035] Among the devices created by multiple research teams is known as robocrop.[1036] This AI-driven robot increases yields by optimizing utility and consistency.[1037] It lines up crop tools precisely and quickly.[1038] A high resolution (HR) and precise system checks the food sector item shrubbery in the framework's forward direction.[1039] The outstanding performance computer analyzes the captured picture to ensure that the green band of photons closest to the crop boundary gets the most attention.[1040] The input devices and processing lines capture a large area, resulting in excellent center-line tracking for crops.[1041] It compares the picture to a real-world field design with crop boundary section.[1042] Collected data is used to position the tools in the row using a hydraulic shift.[1043] The pattern-based characteristic promotes network health and prevents infestations.[1044] Using several cameras and sensors boosts performance and production

---

[1026] Ibid.
[1027] Ibid.
[1028] Ibid.
[1029] Ibid.
[1030] Ibid.
[1031] Ibid.
[1032] Ibid.
[1033] Ibid.
[1034] Ibid.
[1035] Ibid., p. 3
[1036] Ibid.
[1037] Ibid.
[1038] Ibid.
[1039] Ibid.
[1040] Ibid.
[1041] Ibid.
[1042] Ibid.
[1043] Ibid.
[1044] Ibid.

rates.[1045] Harvesting robots have significantly enhanced output in recent decades.[1046] The systems gained popularity because of their advancements and advantages, including increased productivity and reduced worker force.[1047] The dual-arm robot is optimized for fruit harvesting and uses support vector machines (SVM).[1048] Robotic weeding in agriculture automates and effectively controls weeds in crop rows.[1049] The image-processing method was created to recognize crops at various stages of development for autonomous weed management.[1050] Adaptive Robotic Chassis (ARC) is a strawberry flower-specific system.[1051] The device uses an installed camera to catch and process strawberry blooms.[1052] After obtaining the desired coordinate, the robot performs key actions.[1053] The robocrop's effectiveness depends solely on the features in the source picture.[1054] Source images with dominating attributes yield better results.[1055] For each input image sample, the crop should have more shrubs than wildflowers and be close to the RGB color band's mean.[1056] Robocrop systems typically include a console, a hydraulic shaft, a three-point linkage frame, a high-definition camera, speed sensors, and an ADC adaptor.[1057]

Learning frameworks are created to track and predict numerous impacts of nature on agricultural productivity, including fluctuations in the weather.[1058] ML algorithms play an essential role.[1059] ML algorithms, in conjunction using communications satellites, analyze agricultural sustainability, forecast weather conditions, and evaluate farms to determine illnesses and pests.[1060] The framework is excellent at supplying excellent information or data that is constantly revised at a rapid pace.[1061] Furthermore, the company is highly trustworthy in the information it provides to its customers, with periodic use of over a billion layers of agricultural information.[1062] Predictive analysis is based on sources of data like rainfall, wind velocity, solar radiation, and humidity, as well as previous trends.[1063]

[1045] Ibid.
[1046] Ibid.
[1047] Ibid.
[1048] Ibid.
[1049] Ibid.
[1050] Ibid.
[1051] Ibid.
[1052] Ibid.
[1053] Ibid.
[1054] Ibid.
[1055] Ibid.
[1056] Ibid.
[1057] Ibid.
[1058] Ibid.
[1059] Ibid.
[1060] Ibid.
[1061] Ibid.
[1062] Ibid.
[1063] Ibid.

This study plays a crucial role in optimizing crop choices and scheduling for specific agricultural yield.[1064]

FarmShots, a Raleigh, North Carolina-based AI startup, analyzes agricultural data from drone and satellite images.[1065] The company's primary aim aims to identify diseases, pests, and poor nutrition for plants on fields.[1066] In April 2017, the company blocked unlimited entry to their goods for John Deere clients until June 2017.[1067] This alliance demonstrates John Deere's growing interest in agriculture technology freedom.[1068]

In the food processing sector, among the greatest laborious and difficult duties for production facilities is accurate food product ordering and packing.[1069] As a consequence, AI-based machines may handle this kind of tiresome procedure, minimizing the likelihood of mistake and raising the sector's production pace swiftly.[1070] The development of AI-generated systems is strenuous because of the abnormalities in the colors, shapes, and sizes of fruits and vegetables.[1071] Creating an AI-powered arranging and packing process requires extensive data collection to ensure efficient training and performance.[1072] Multiple teams of researchers developed multiple systems with an identical purpose.[1073] TOMRA is a highly efficient sorting algorithm.[1074] It enhanced production accuracy by 90%.[1075] Today, automated systems do a great deal of merchandise packaging and sorting tasks.[1076] Using these methods can lead to increased production costs, larger yields, and cheaper expenses for labor.[1077]

AI-powered smart systems for making decisions use numerous methods and instruments, including superior resolution photographic equipment, laser-technology-based structures, X-ray-based structures, and infrared spectrum.[1078] Such techniques and advancements are utilized to

---

[1064] Ibid.
[1065] Ibid.
[1066] Ibid.
[1067] Ibid.
[1068] Ibid.
[1069] Ibid., p. 4
[1070] Ibid.
[1071] Ibid.
[1072] Ibid.
[1073] Ibid.
[1074] Ibid.
[1075] Ibid.
[1076] Ibid.
[1077] Ibid.
[1078] Ibid.

assess each component of agricultural goods, including vegetables and fruits, on the source level.[1079] Traditional methods are limited to identifying excellent and undesirable goods according to their appearance.[1080] TOMRA was shown to improve detachment and organizing problems in potatoes by 5-10%.[1081] A Japanese corporation successfully solved a similar challenge using a TensorFlow ML-based solution, resulting in significant benefits for their assembly unit.[1082] This technique has proven effective in various food processing industries.[1083] Additionally, every business noticed that the AI-powered system performs with greater precision.[1084] The achievement of AI-based technologies on spuds paves the way for other applications.[1085] It can be tailored to certain sectors or departments within the food processing business.[1086]

The KanKan and Shanghai local healthcare office collaborated together to create an AI-based system that recognizes objects and faces anonymously.[1087] This technique aims to track persons whom disregard food manufacturing unit sanitary rules, which were implemented in various countries, including the USA.[1088]

AI is benefiting both food processing businesses and customers in selecting unique flavors.[1089] Kellogg's debuted Bear Naked-Custom in 2018, enabling consumers to personalize the granola with more than 50 ingredients.[1090] The system records individual preferences for flavors, client tastes, and other relevant information.[1091] This knowledge is critical for successfully releasing an innovative item into the hands of consumers.[1092] AI helped design effective decision-making processes for customers.[1093]

For the food manufacturing sector, thorough maintenance and cleaning of manufacturing machinery is critical.[1094] AI-powered systems can readily handle such a task. Several sensors and

---

[1079] Ibid.
[1080] Ibid.
[1081] Ibid.
[1082] Ibid.
[1083] Ibid.
[1084] Ibid.
[1085] Ibid.
[1086] Ibid.
[1087] Ibid.
[1088] Ibid.
[1089] Ibid.
[1090] Ibid.
[1091] Ibid.
[1092] Ibid.
[1093] Ibid.
[1094] Ibid., p. 5

cameras are used to finish the operation.[1095] Each of Whitwell and Martec's products has muscle weakness, which allows for high efficiency in a short period of time.[1096] Currently, Martec is attempting to defend its AI-based washing station concept.[1097] Towards this strategy, Martec uses ultrasound sensor technologies for imaging and fluorescent light ways to grow the received data for AI system development.[1098] The equipment monitors residual microbial and food debris.[1099] The system will take stand after the entire evaluation result is released.[1100]

Launching up-to-date items for any production unit is a time-consuming undertaking.[1101] The consumer's interests are paramount, particularly in the food industry.[1102] As a result, the data obtained by various systems that make decisions for clients is useful for the launch of novel products.[1103] The ML-based component analyzes collected information and generates relevant product decisions.[1104] Topics like "what customers are exactly looking for" were solved utilizing an ML-based method.[1105] AI is currently used in the area of food processing and packaging industries to develop new goods.[1106] Formerly, this task was done via a report or polls, resulting in a poor success rate for the system.[1107] However, AI and ML are now widely employed for similar tasks.[1108]

Coca-Cola has erected a self-service soft drink area, known as Coca-Cola Freestyle, in the United States.[1109] This allows users to create hundreds of cocktails with slight flavor adjustments.[1110] The system records this type of activity and then uses ML and DL algorithms for further analysis.[1111] Using this information, novel goods may be introduced.[1112] Cherry Sprite is an immediate form product concept.[1113] The food industry might employ algorithmic recommendations to

---

[1095] Ibid.
[1096] Ibid.
[1097] Ibid.
[1098] Ibid.
[1099] Ibid.
[1100] Ibid.
[1101] Ibid.
[1102] Ibid.
[1103] Ibid.
[1104] Ibid.
[1105] Ibid.
[1106] Ibid.
[1107] Ibid.
[1108] Ibid.
[1109] Ibid.
[1110] Ibid.
[1111] Ibid.
[1112] Ibid.
[1113] Ibid.

generate novel commodities in the decades to come.[1114]

Food industries must be transparent about the supply chain of food goods as they prioritize food safety policies.[1115] AI is used to track the whole procedure.[1116] This covers anything including price control to stock control.[1117] This forecasts and monitors the journey of possessions from their origin until consumer collection.[1118] Symphony Retail offers AI-powered booking, billing, and inventory management capabilities.[1119] It promotes discipline and prevents overconsumption, which can lead to exhausted materials.[1120]

According to Sachani, et al. (2021), AI and automation may enhance convenient mart kitchen food service revenues.[1121] Automation and AI are rapidly altering several industries, including food service.[1122] Convenient marts, which have traditionally focused on rapid, convenient shopping, are increasingly utilizing new technologies to improve their food service.[1123] This trend is driven by revenue growth and increased operational efficiency.[1124] As consumer demand for fast, high-quality, and personalized meals grows, AI and automation in convenience store kitchens may increase profitability.[1125] Technology is very beneficial to convenience store food service companies.[1126]

Convenient marts cater to a varied and transient consumer base seeking quick and high-quality service.[1127] Automation and AI can improve kitchen operations, cut wait times, and assure consistent food preparation, leading to a better customer experience.[1128] To meet modern customer expectations and operational efficiency, the food service process must be redesigned rather than simply incorporating new technologies.[1129] AI innovations like ML and statistical analysis are critical

---

[1114] Ibid.

[1115] Ibid.

[1116] Ibid.

[1117] Ibid.

[1118] Ibid.

[1119] Ibid.

[1120] Ibid.

[1121] Sachani, Dipakkumar Kanubhai, Niravkumar Dhameliya, Kishore Mullangi, Sunil Kumar Anumandla, and Sai Charan Vennapusa. "Enhancing Food Service Sales through AI and Automation in Convenience Store Kitchens." *Global Disclosure of Economics and Business* 10, no. 2 (December 31, 2021): p. 105. https://doi.org/10.18034/gdeb.v10i2.754.

[1122] Ibid.

[1123] Ibid.

[1124] Ibid.

[1125] Ibid.

[1126] Ibid.

[1127] Ibid.

[1128] Ibid.

[1129] Ibid.

to this transformation.[1130] Convenient marts use these technology to manage inventory, estimate demand, and tailor customer experiences.[1131] Predictive analytics can optimize staffing and inventory levels during peak hours, reducing waste and improving service speed.[1132] ML algorithms optimize product mix and sales by analyzing purchasing trends and recommending popular menu items.[1133]

Automation and AI handle tiresome jobs, allowing staff to focus on more important duties.[1134] Convenient mart kitchens utilize robotic process automation (RPA) for inventory management, self-service kiosks, and automated cooking equipment.[1135] Automated cooking equipment improves food preparation accuracy and reduces human mistake.[1136] Self-service kiosks use AI to provide personalized recommendations and expedite orders.[1137] Convenient mart kitchen automation and AI integration address specific food service concerns.[1138] Automation can decrease repetitive labor in convenient marts, addressing the labor issue.[1139] Precision and efficiency of these technologies can lead to cost savings and increased profitability.[1140] AI and automated systems disclose consumer preferences as well as operational effectiveness.[1141]

Convenient marts have faced challenges in adapting to shifting consumer preferences and company demands.[1142] These pressures are especially obvious in the food service industry.[1143] Convenient marts offer convenience and a diverse range, but their food service operations are generally inefficient, unreliable, and limited in scalability.[1144] These challenges are exacerbated by a lack of staff, changing consumer demands, and the requirement for fast service.[1145] Convenient mart kitchen management must match consumer demands for speedy, high-quality, and customizable cuisine.[1146]

[1130] Ibid., p. 106
[1131] Ibid.
[1132] Ibid.
[1133] Ibid.
[1134] Ibid.
[1135] Ibid.
[1136] Ibid.
[1137] Ibid.
[1138] Ibid.
[1139] Ibid.
[1140] Ibid.
[1141] Ibid.
[1142] Ibid.
[1143] Ibid.
[1144] Ibid.
[1145] Ibid.
[1146] Ibid.

According to Adak, Pradham, and Shukla (2022), the growth of food delivery service (FDS) apps during the COVID-19 pandemic has provided flexibility and a range of eateries for the convenience and comfort of households and businesses.[1147] Increased immigration from many nations has led in the introduction of new cuisines to the country.[1148] Customers are given various meal alternatives and flexibility to place orders from the greatest cafes or eateries in the area, whether their residence or at work.[1149] Despite apps being a normal feature on smartphones and tablets and the global positioning system (GPS) being widely accessible, delivering meals to a client's specific place is hardly a problem.[1150] Consumers can monitor their order's progress from placing it to receiving it.[1151] As meal takeaway services become more popular, digital marketplaces are expanding their offerings.[1152]

International food ordering and delivery platforms, such as Uber Eats in the United States, Deliveroo in the United Kingdom, and Menulog in Australia, use a cost-intensive business strategy but are responsible for all delivery logistics.[1153] These organizations provide an entire marketing aid to restaurant owners at no additional cost and operate on the commission basis.[1154] Meal delivery apps such as DoorDash and Uber Eats, restaurants have to charge listing fees to restaurants while many locally-owned delivery apps do not charge restaurants to list. Using a couple of phone taps, FDS apps take requests, collect up meals at food establishments, and then bring it to the consumer.[1155] A chain of restaurants provides customers with various dining options.[1156] Customers are hungry for such services, which is great news for online food providers.[1157] Despite forecasts that Australia's meal delivery industry would expand, COVID-19 quarantines and lockdowns resulted in a spike in FDSs, especially apps developed by third parties such as Uber Eats, Deliveroo, and Menulog, as customers are compelled to purchase electronically while eateries were closed.[1158] Given a rise in transactions and comments, many businesses seek to efficiently utilize information to identify opportunities for

---

[1147] Adak, Anirban, Biswajeet Pradhan, and Nagesh Shukla. "Sentiment Analysis of Customer Reviews of Food Delivery Services Using Deep Learning and Explainable Artificial Intelligence: Systematic Review." *Foods* 11, no. 10 (May 21, 2022): 1500. https://doi.org/10.3390/foods11101500.

[1148] Ibid.
[1149] Ibid.
[1150] Ibid.
[1151] Ibid.
[1152] Ibid.
[1153] Ibid.
[1154] Ibid.
[1155] Ibid.
[1156] Ibid.
[1157] Ibid.
[1158] Ibid.

development and boost client happiness.[1159]

Consumer emotion may be seen in blogging entries, feedback, evaluations, or social media posts that discuss meal value, customer service, time of arrival, among other topics.[1160] FDS firms can perceive what their consumers are stating and interpret favorable remarks as compliments and negative feedback as complaints.[1161] Topic modeling can be used to categorize negative attitudes into several complaint groups.[1162] Customer experiences with meals can change depending on the season, including a spike in favorable feedback during the busy season.[1163] With large sales and expenditures, FDS businesses keep having difficulty with revenue due to rising costs.[1164] Competitive pricing is a frequent approach for heating the competitive market, in which enterprises absorb a loss in sales by heavily discounting dining expenses.[1165] In addition, internet FDS have limited oversight of the quality of food and are heavily reliant on eateries.[1166] If the consumer is disappointed with food quality, the meal delivery company must absorb the profit loss.[1167] As a consequence, firms such as Sprig and Munchery were incapable of withstanding the decline in revenue and have ceased operations.[1168] Tracking client feedback and ratings is the sole method for FDS to guarantee that the delivery operation provides a positive customer experience while not negatively impacting the dine-in experience.[1169]

According to Patel (2024), AI is revolutionizing the online meal delivery sector by influencing what people buy and guaranteeing that the food comes hot and fresh.[1170] DoorDash employs AI to customize suggestions, forecast variations in demand, and improve routes for delivery.[1171] Their AI-powered "DashPass" membership plan provides users tailored prices along with complimentary delivery depending on their personal tastes.[1172] Grubhub uses AI for price optimization, to guarantee eateries are fairly compensated throughout busy periods and that customers receive the greatest rates

---

[1159] Ibid.
[1160] Ibid.
[1161] Ibid.
[1162] Ibid.
[1163] Ibid.
[1164] Ibid.
[1165] Ibid.
[1166] Ibid.
[1167] Ibid.
[1168] Ibid.
[1169] Ibid.
[1170] Ibid.
[1171] Ibid.
[1172] Ibid.

throughout non-peak times.[1173] Moreover, their AI-powered chatbots manage a large number of consumer inquiries, boosting response times and lowering customer care expenses.[1174] Uber Eats employs AI to maximize routes for delivery and dynamic pricing.[1175] They additionally use AI-powered "voice ordering" technologies to deliver a seamless customer interaction.[1176]

As AI advances, users should anticipate further imaginative uses in the meal delivery industry.[1177] Predictive ordering, driverless delivery, and hyper-personalization are some of the fascinating possibilities.[1178] AI will anticipate consumer needs depending on variables such as the time of day, weather, and special occasions.[1179] While autonomous transportation is nonetheless in its infancy, AI-powered drones and autonomous cars have a chance to transform distribution of food by drastically lowering times for delivery and prices.[1180] AI will extend its reach beyond meal suggestions to customize the overall customer experience.[1181] Applications would recommend specific cuisines according to the environment, or eateries depending on the individual's present attitude.[1182]

AI is not merely a future idea, rather a strong technology influencing the meal delivery sector.[1183] AI is making food delivery quicker, far more accessible, and eventually enjoyable to all consumers by customizing the consumer experience, improving processes, and opening up new opportunities.[1184] As AI technology advances, meal delivery apps will become ever more intelligent, efficient, and pleasurable.[1185]

[1173] Ibid.
[1174] Ibid.
[1175] Ibid.
[1176] Ibid.
[1177] Ibid.
[1178] Ibid.
[1179] Ibid.
[1180] Ibid.
[1181] Ibid.
[1182] Ibid.
[1183] Ibid.
[1184] Ibid.
[1185] Ibid.

6 AI AND THE PRESS

Kreps, McCain, and Brundage (2020) found that the 2016 US presidential election highlighted how foreign players may impact news coverage, the public's assessment of political candidates, and election results.[1186] Digital hyper-targeting, which targets specific groups to influence political preferences, has led to in restrictions on political advertising on social media platforms like X (formerly Twitter).[1187] A 2019 US Senate committee investigating foreign involvement in American elections advised the government to, "reinforce with the public the danger of attempted foreign interference in elections."[1188] The remark implies that the public can protect itself from meddling, but only if they are alert and cautious about disseminating false information.[1189]

By the exact same time, the congressional committee observed that Russian attempts to influence are becoming "more sophisticated" with tactics which could undermine the capacity of the public to distinguish fact from fabrication.[1190] In fact, cutting-edge AI technology is currently producing writing which closely resembles the formatting and content of actual media items, whilst avoiding the space constraints that humans have when creating text.[1191] When such frameworks allow fraudulent individuals to create and release credible-sounding headlines on a broad basis, the possibility of misinformation, defined as "false or misleading information," increases: the volume of fake news might skyrocket, and the ease of writing production may allow for coordinated hypertargeting

---

[1186] Kreps, Sarah, R. Miles McCain, and Miles Brundage. "All the News That's Fit to Fabricate: AI-Generated Text as a Tool of Media Misinformation." *Journal of Experimental Political Science* 9, no. 1 (2020): p. 104. https://doi.org/10.1017/xps.2020.37.

[1187] Ibid., p. 104-105

[1188] Ibid., p. 105

[1189] Ibid.

[1190] Ibid.

[1191] Ibid.

of pieces to specific organizations.[1192] Nevertheless, assuming the general population rejects fake news reports, democratic institutions face minimal harm from these technologies.[1193]

According to Rothman (2025), news reporting has been steadily becoming more negative over time.[1194] It is clear that not every issue has gotten progressively more serious during the last 80 years.[1195] This is taking place outside of the real world, instead within the media sector, and because a person's image of society outside his or her personal knowledge has been drastically formed by the media, its increasing pessimism is significant.[1196]

According to the US Bureau of Labor Statistics, less than 50,000 individuals worked as reporters in 2023, and this is lower than the number of individuals who deliver for DoorDash in New York City—and this tiny crew is tasked with an insurmountable challenge of producing an imposing and intriguing account of a confusing world on a daily basis.[1197] Reporters assist the greater interest with revealing unsettling realities, and their job helps to better community.[1198] However, the further unpleasant realities emerge, the more dire situations appear.[1199] Subscribers cringe at the harshness of reports, yet they read upon frightening or disturbing headlines in higher numbers—so media outlets, including those that aim towards honesty and independence, possess a motivation to cause concern their target viewers.[1200] Subscribers grumble against the partisanship of the headlines, yet they engage in stories which appear to support their opinions on politics.[1201] It was unsurprising that individuals trusted journalists less.[1202] The days of feeling informed by reading the front page of the newspaper and watching a 30-minute newscast awaiting "The Tonight Show" to begin are long gone.[1203] However, there is one positive aspect of the news: it has the potential to change.[1204]

There is no doubt that change is on the way.[1205] AI is already changing the way people create,

---

[1192] Ibid.

[1193] Ibid.

[1194] Rothman, Joshua. "Will A.I. Save the News?" The New Yorker, April 8, 2025. https://www.newyorker.com/culture/open-questions/will-ai-save-the-news.

[1195] Ibid.

[1196] Ibid.

[1197] Ibid.

[1198] Ibid.

[1199] Ibid.

[1200] Ibid.

[1201] Ibid.

[1202] Ibid.

[1203] Ibid.

[1204] Ibid.

[1205] Ibid.

distribute, and consume news, both on the need and supply sides.[1206] AI highlights headlines, allowing people to consume less; but may additionally be employed to create stories.[1207] Today, for example, Google selects whether to offer someone an "AI overview" that extracts information from news pieces and includes links to the source material.[1208] AI voices read a computer-generated screenplay on the science-and-technology podcast "Discovery Daily," a stand-alone news product released by Perplexity, an AI search firm.[1209]

Summarization's continual growth may make human writers—with their distinct personalities, experiences, viewpoints, and insights—more valuable, both in comparison to and as part of the AI ecosystem.[1210] It is also possible that AI will bring up new opportunities in newsrooms.[1211] Because reporters would be in control, they may utilize it to advance the truthful reporting of new facts while keeping a news organization's crucial commitment to being a trusted source of truth.[1212]

However, there is no way around the financial issues.[1213] While consumers respect reporters who are human and the outcomes they create, consumers might also appreciate media organizations— the writers, producers, creators, and entrepreneurs who support AI individual voices may survive while corporations perish as AI advances.[1214] In this instance, the headlines could have emptied away.[1215] Consumers might be stuck with AI-summarized news feeds instead of anything else.[1216]

Information spreads via media such as Facebook that is also influenced by AI.[1217] This is simple to observe why AI-generated posts will revolutionize text-centric platforms like X and Facebook; as generative video develops, so will video-based sites like YouTube, TikTok, and Twitch.[1218] This could grow increasingly impossible to distinguish amongst actual and fraudulent people—which sounds bad.[1219] However, the repercussions remain unresolved.[1220] AI-based content may find an

---

[1206] Ibid.
[1207] Ibid.
[1208] Ibid.
[1209] Ibid.
[1210] Ibid.
[1211] Ibid.
[1212] Ibid.
[1213] Ibid.
[1214] Ibid.
[1215] Ibid.
[1216] Ibid.
[1217] Ibid.
[1218] Ibid.
[1219] Ibid.
[1220] Ibid.

eager social media audience.[1221]

What AI enables is an algorithm which distinguishes style from information.[1222] A big model of language may absorb knowledge within a single structure, fully comprehend what it means, and then pour that knowledge to a different mold.[1223] Previously, just an individual person might extract concepts through a newspaper article, a work of literature, or a speech and clarify those concepts to someone else, frequently using a traditional method known as "conversation."[1224] This process can now be simplified.[1225] It is like knowledge was compressed, allowing it to flow with greater ease.[1226] Unfortunately, mistakes might occur throughout this process.[1227]

It is easy to argue as the AI result is simply representing data which currently present.[1228] However, the ability of redevelopment—the ability to instruct an AI, "do it again, a little differently"—should not be overlooked.[1229] The identical post or clip may be reproduced and published in various versions and tastes, enabling users or computers to select those that best fit their needs.[1230] Today, if a person is interested in fixing anything within their residence, he or she may be quite assured that someone, somewhere, has created a YouTube video detailing how to do so; the same rationale may soon apply to the news.[1231]

Around exactly the same a period of time the fluidity of AI might be effective contrary to social networking sites.[1232] Customization may enable a person to bypass the steps of investigating, identifying, and distributing entirely; about a short time, an AI may be able to make a podcast covering the news stories that he or she is most interested in.[1233] If someone enjoys a specific human-created podcast—say, "Radiolab" or "Pod Save America"—an AI may be capable to modify it on behalf of a reader, pinching and folding it till it goes inside a person's 24-minute commute.[1234]

[1221] Ibid.
[1222] Ibid.
[1223] Ibid.
[1224] Ibid.
[1225] Ibid.
[1226] Ibid.
[1227] Ibid.
[1228] Ibid.
[1229] Ibid.
[1230] Ibid.
[1231] Ibid.
[1232] Ibid.
[1233] Ibid.
[1234] Ibid.

The varied quality and dubious veracity of AI news now protects skilled news enterprises.[1235] As the years go by and AI advances, many types of users might discover novel methods to embrace it.[1236] People who like social networking might upon AI stories.[1237] A few individuals are currently performing the aforementioned, on TikTok and others.[1238] Individuals who do not use platforms such as Facebook might turn to bots or other AI resources, while others may opt for stories which are openly positioned as mixing human reporters with AI.[1239] Individuals might favor the traditional model, whereby people generate separate bits of well-vetted, thoroughly fact-checked news and publish them individually.[1240]

According to Pachal (2025), when people discuss whether AI may transform the press, the word "hyper-personalization" comes up frequently.[1241] In general terms, it means that AI may personalize the experience to a user's preferences—as long as it has enough information about that person.[1242] At a certain level, computers and advertising technology were accomplishing it over decades by suggesting sites or articles according to a user's actions and past browsing habits.[1243]

Generative AI gives the power to alter the content.[1244] A large model of language might, hypothetically, identify the types of tales that people are interested in and adjust what they are reading—perhaps by adding a regional perspective.[1245] It could even provide various lengths and formats.[1246]

Verbal features like ChatGPT's Advanced Voice Mode are appropriate for that particular purpose.[1247] If a person does not participate within a meeting to brainstorm when commuting or jogging, he or she is missing out.[1248] When it comes to brainstorming, AI can be a great help.[1249] Even

---

[1235] Ibid.

[1236] Ibid.

[1237] Ibid.

[1238] Ibid.

[1239] Ibid.

[1240] Ibid.

[1241] Pachal, Pete. "The next Big AI Shift in Media? Turning News into a Two-Way Conversation." Fast Company, April 11, 2025. https://www.fastcompany.com/91314614/how-ai-is-transforming-news-into-a-two-way-conversation.

[1242] Ibid.

[1243] Ibid.

[1244] Ibid.

[1245] Ibid.

[1246] Ibid.

[1247] Ibid.

[1248] Ibid.

[1249] Ibid.

better, it can be an excellent writing helper, assisting you in developing ideas, staying on course, and filling in the gaps in your arguments—all without taking over the writing itself.[1250]

Apply the same principle to how people consume news.[1251] Whenever a reader reaches a place in the novel where he or she wants to delve deeper, he or she can do so right away.[1252] If a person reads a story on getting the terrible wolf back after its disappearance, he or she may wonder if the same approach could be used to additional extinct animals, whether philosophers are reacting, or the way the story affects the biotechnology industry.[1253] AI could integrate every aspect of this information sans having to "navigate" everything.[1254]

People may have noticed preliminary indicators of this type of conduct.[1255] For instance, users frequently tag Grok on X, the platform's bot, with additional inquiries regarding current topics.[1256] This represents a subtle yet significant conduct: rather than simply perusing the headlines, consumers automatically use it as a springboard into more substantive discussion.[1257] Many story pieces seek to present the most up-to-date information, with only a little background provided at the finale.[1258] This frequently makes sophisticated subjects, such as Bitcoin, inaccessible to casual readers.[1259] A news report, on the other hand, may operate like a discussion, explaining topics precisely at a person's level of comprehension.[1260] In other words, the most effective customizing technique is not data, but the reader's words.[1261] The only hitch is that AI must change from giving people things to assisting them in discovering things for themselves.[1262] The reader must be educated on how to use AI.[1263]

However, context is important in making that vision of AI and journalism work: In other words, machines still require a map.[1264] To deliver a person the absolute best information for whichever news

---

[1250] Ibid.
[1251] Ibid.
[1252] Ibid.
[1253] Ibid.
[1254] Ibid.
[1255] Ibid.
[1256] Ibid.
[1257] Ibid.
[1258] Ibid.
[1259] Ibid.
[1260] Ibid.
[1261] Ibid.
[1262] Ibid.
[1263] Ibid.
[1264] Ibid.

rabbit hole someone wishes to travel down, AI need a data collection that is focused on news subjects.[1265] The enormous data sets in today's large language models are likely overkill, as they introduce noise or generic information when specificity is required.[1266] However, limiting the context to only the content on the website that a person is reading would be too restrictive.[1267]

A better option would be to create a "general news corpus" of approved sources that publishers may choose to use and that other sites could access to provide a broad context for their AI experiences.[1268] ProRata and NewsGuard are developing similar technologies, however their primary use case may not be universal search engines like Perplexity or ProRata's own Gist.[1269] Context is perhaps more crucial when a reader has already clicked on an article and started down a route.[1270] With AI, that path does not have to be linear; the reader can travel in any direction and the appropriate context will follow.[1271]

The most attractive aspect of this vision of individualized news is that it does not require Big Tech involvement, at least not beyond the development of big language models.[1272] Journalists give the raw data, product designers create the experiences, and third-party content brokers compile the context.[1273]

For the past 20 years, media corporations have optimized their platforms by attempting to predict how viewers will respond.[1274] However, AI may render that technique obsolete.[1275] Imagine a news experience in which every reader receives the background they require, the angles they care about, and the context to delve deeper—all by just asking.[1276] That is not personalization through prediction.[1277] That is personalizing through involvement.[1278]

According to Caswell and Fitzgerald (2025), despite all of this ambiguity, something is certain: AI

[1265] Ibid.
[1266] Ibid.
[1267] Ibid.
[1268] Ibid.
[1269] Ibid.
[1270] Ibid.
[1271] Ibid.
[1272] Ibid.
[1273] Ibid.
[1274] Ibid.
[1275] Ibid.
[1276] Ibid.
[1277] Ibid.
[1278] Ibid.

is disrupting journalism—rearranging anything between the way news is received, made, and transmitted to the definition of what the word "news" actually implies.[1279] AI remains flawed, yet it can comprehend and compose, speak and listen, ingest, generate, synthesize, and contextualize knowledge at breakneck rate and effectiveness, outperforming conventional reporters, writers, and strategists.[1280] This has become the principal issue of conversation in newspaper and broadcaster boardrooms.[1281] Many proceed with extreme care, and other people are pouring in.[1282]

Many attempts at incorporating AI are concentrated on rather prosaic duties—copyediting, summarizing, and producing stories—which would have of been known to journalists in the 1700s.[1283] Few mention the probability of AI could profoundly alter ways communities and humans perceive the globe.[1284] It will impact everyone, not just the journalism sector.[1285] Take "generative search," which Google and others introduced in 2024.[1286] It offers serious risks to the industry because it almost eliminates the need for internet users to visit numerous news sites by providing brief, AI-generated responses to inquiries like "who started the First World War?"[1287] If not handled properly, these new capabilities have the potential to spread lies and distortions on a scale never seen before.[1288] Consider the technology giants and Trump's inauguration, and picture how such capabilities could be utilized for questions like "Who was responsible for the January 6th attack on the Capitol?"[1289]

Instead of generating articles or clips for numerous viewers, AI-powered machines can generate stories tailored to each person.[1290] An appropriate analogy would be if every piece of music on the streaming service Spotify was synthetically generated for each listener, adapted to their specific preferences, rather than being produced by an artist for a huge audience.[1291] Ultra-personalized news may address increasing news prevention, but it is also transitory, no trace left behind.[1292] If neglected,

---

[1279] Caswell, David, and Mary Fitzgerald. "AI Is the Media's Chance to Reinvent Itself." AI is the media's chance to reinvent itself, March 5, 2025. https://www.prospectmagazine.co.uk/ideas/media/69423/artificial-intelligence-journalism-reinvention.

[1280] Ibid.
[1281] Ibid.
[1282] Ibid.
[1283] Ibid.
[1284] Ibid.
[1285] Ibid.
[1286] Ibid.
[1287] Ibid.
[1288] Ibid.
[1289] Ibid.
[1290] Ibid.
[1291] Ibid.
[1292] Ibid.

this will swiftly eliminate whatever remains of common truths.[1293] The common arena could disappear, rendering the globe significantly fractured and polarized.[1294]

The news industry has a dismal track record of responding to severe upheavals.[1295] During the late 1990s and early 2000s, when technological firms seemed eager to capitalize on the burgeoning internet's evident long-term opportunities, bloggers, online communities, search engines, and audio- and video-on-demand largely underwhelmed newspapers, magazine publishers, and broadcasters.[1296] Social media usage was regarded as a small advertising medium, most effectively handled by interns and novel reporters.[1297] As the point that the enormous impact of these fresh kinds of communication became clear, it had been past time for the majority of news outlets to play anything besides a submissive role to digital networks.[1298]   Massive sections of this sector was annihilated and "news deserts" (in which individuals lack the ability to obtain regional news) emerged, having numerous consequences for society.[1299] Over 50% of US counties had no or little regional media coverage; in the United Kingdom, over 320 regional publications shuttered from 2009 to 2019, with revenue from advertising falling 70% over the time.[1300] Generative AI, fueled by a multibillion-dollar investment increase, is expected to result in even more profound developments.[1301] Journalism organizations must make an unavoidable choice: would they employ AI to replace their existing labor clinging to established methods and goods, but would they take note of the errors of the previous great technological disruption and rethink journalism entirely?[1302]

The profession of public-interest reporting includes, amongst other duties, determining the authenticity of knowledge prior to publication and amending the facts if it is found to be erroneous.[1303] Every day, reporting creates an inaccurate but persistent chronicle of events which is archived in text, audio, and video.[1304] This record has been verified; it can be cited, challenged, amended, clarified, and circulated among numerous individuals.[1305] Its genesis is proven

---

[1293] Ibid.
[1294] Ibid.
[1295] Ibid.
[1296] Ibid.
[1297] Ibid.
[1298] Ibid.
[1299] Ibid.
[1300] Ibid.
[1301] Ibid.
[1302] Ibid.
[1303] Ibid.
[1304] Ibid.
[1305] Ibid.

and accounted for.[1306] AI-mediated media networks, such as X-Stories, provide none of these features.[1307] The following does not mean to argue that AI systems are unable to benefit society.[1308] Cuestión Pública, a Colombian news organization, developed a language model that uses journalistic investigation and organized information to quickly convey verified current events.[1309] Instead of simply copying standard media types, the journalism industry is drawing younger viewers by gaming, parodying on Hollywood and Netflix blockbusters ("Game of Votes" and "I Know What You Did Last Legislative Term") to uncover political wrongdoing.[1310] Scrolla.Africa, a news service in southern Africa, implemented an AI technology to assist grassroots journalists in reporting stories in eloquent and readily available forms.[1311] Thousands more prototypes and trials like these are currently underway worldwide.[1312] However, a lot of the media of today misses the creativity and tolerance for risk required to rethink the media's capability to correct itself and pursue authenticity at volume in the AI era—and is not controlled or driven by eccentric billionaires like Elon Musk.[1313]

Vesala (2022) argues that the Directive on Copyright in the Digital Single Market failed to consider AI impact on press publishers' rights, despite its growing significance.[1314] The application of copyright to AI-based news output has become a topic of interest, as concerns regarding its status arise.[1315] To achieve the goal of journalistic promotion and editorial investment, AI impact on news production terms must be considered when applying the press publishers' right to news content produced with or without AI.[1316]

According to Posada, Weller, and Wong (2021), society is currently in the datafication era.[1317] The term "datafication" refers to the digital processing, quantification, and storage of the world, as well as

---

[1306] Ibid.

[1307] Ibid.

[1308] Ibid.

[1309] Ibid.

[1310] Ibid.

[1311] Ibid.

[1312] Ibid.

[1313] Ibid.

[1314] Vesala, Juha. "Press Publishers Right and Artificial Intelligence." *Artificial Intelligence and the Media*, February 15, 2022, p. 240. https://doi.org/10.4337/9781839109973.00018.

[1315] Ibid.

[1316] Ibid., p. 240-241

[1317] Posada, Julian, Nicholas Weller, and Wendy H. Wong. "We Haven't Gone Paperless yet: Why the Printing Press Can Help Us Understand Data and AI." *Proceedings of the 2021 AAAI/ACM Conference on AI, Ethics, and Society*, July 21, 2021, p. 864. https://doi.org/10.1145/3461702.3462604.

its conversion into binary code.[1318] The proliferation of AI technology has been a significant advance in datafication.[1319] The emergence of "Big Data" being absent, information-intensive ML algorithms would not have made the great advances which they have made and remains to make.[1320] Given the surge in gathering and analyzing information and access, humans have battled to establish strategies for data governance, AI regulation, and articulating the political and social implications of data collection and AI.[1321] There are many questions regarding the breadth and ethics of data, but few clear answers have emerged.[1322]

However, datafication also resulted in a growing power centralization, with individuals who devised the methods to collect information more efficiently and broadly gaining disproportionate authority.[1323] Social networking sites, such as Facebook and X, aim to gather information which has grown to control how individuals engage with free speech.[1324] The decision to enable Trump and his allies to spread falsehoods during his first term, as well as the decision to sever him following the January 6, 2021 Capitol riots, highlighted this issue.[1325] Search engines like Google and online retailers like Amazon influence the way individuals view the globe as well as what they can obtain.[1326] These changes began to accelerate after the COVID-19 pandemic started.[1327]

Analogies with printing equipment may assist us to comprehend how datafication and AI may transform livelihood.[1328] The printing equipment dramatically altered things in earlier society as well as politics in three distinct manners that remain valid now.[1329] First, it shifted society's spoken orientation to visual orientation.[1330] It made conversation more meditative rather than collaborative.[1331] It additionally dedicated thoughts to writing as an instrument with unique setting up reasoning for conveying knowledge.[1332] Then, it transferred authority away from the religious community and government as information keepers to individuals.[1333] This restored financial

---

[1318] Ibid.
[1319] Ibid.
[1320] Ibid.
[1321] Ibid.
[1322] Ibid.
[1323] Ibid.
[1324] Ibid.
[1325] Ibid.
[1326] Ibid.
[1327] Ibid.
[1328] Ibid., p. 864-865
[1329] Ibid., p. 865
[1330] Ibid.
[1331] Ibid.
[1332] Ibid.
[1333] Ibid.

objectives and influence, thus strengthening writers and printing devices.[1334] With the rise of newspapers and novels, it became easier to imagine "communities" for humans.[1335] Then, the archive began as a storehouse for certain papers and publications with a social purpose, but has now evolved into an information source, reality, and influence.[1336]

The most major technological advance to take as an analogy is the printing press, which transformed information generation, reception, and utilization, as well as storage.[1337] Like the printing press, datafication dramatically transforms our political and social interactions by storing and sharing data more efficiently.[1338] This facilitates large-scale data collection.[1339] AI is the technique we use to analyze and arrange information; it additionally develops on the data archives.[1340] Firstly, data collection and AI have led to an environment of storing and forecasting, with acts occurring place on computers along with systems that customers cannot understand.[1341] It appears to be more public, but is actually more private in terms of data storage and use.[1342] Second, these factors have moved control beyond governments to individuals that design and control algorithmic processes, as it is these individuals whom create the groups of information to be gathered, as well as apply algorithmic processes to gather and evaluate user information.[1343] Individuals are gaining greater ability to obtain data and knowledge, yet data are acquired from them in various ways, both voluntary and involuntary.[1344] Third, while algorithms have increased chances for community growth, they can also lead to deeper fissures as people are divided into separate "filter bubbles."[1345] Machines are now arbitrators of reality and influence, deciding which information is accessible and by who.[1346]

The datafication economics focuses on the monetary benefits for individuals who generate data from observed reality.[1347] The term "surveillance capitalism" refers to how firms use data to produce

---

[1334] Ibid.
[1335] Ibid.
[1336] Ibid.
[1337] Ibid.
[1338] Ibid.
[1339] Ibid.
[1340] Ibid.
[1341] Ibid.
[1342] Ibid.
[1343] Ibid.
[1344] Ibid.
[1345] Ibid.
[1346] Ibid.
[1347] Ibid.

income while controlling access to information.[1348] Some scholars, such Fourcade and Healy, focus on categorizing consumers based on their data and the moral judgments that come with it.[1349]

The concept of "dataveillance" captures the political and ethical aspects of datafication well.[1350] Dataveillance refers to the monitoring, aggregation, and sifting of data for control purposes.[1351] Dataveillance examines the shadow cast by individuals during economic, social, or political transactions, as opposed to physical monitoring.[1352] Technology allows for more intrusions into people's life, sometimes justified for security reasons.[1353]

According to Monti (2018), reporting and press coverage have historically been heavily affected by technical advances, and this is especially true in the age of technology, compared to the competitiveness of contemporary media and the problems of Web 2.0 to the development of a new approach to make headlines, i.e. automated journalism.[1354] Automated journalism is the utilization of AI, i.e. algorithms, to create news stories with no human involvement, with the exception of programmers who (eventually) developed the software.[1355]

Automated journalism, a subset of post-industrial reporting, refers to the technological problems that reporting encounters.[1356] It entails AI utilization (e.g., software or algorithms) that generates headlines with no human feedback, other than the programmer(s) who created the algorithm.[1357] An AI algorithm gathers and analyzes information before writing a news item.[1358] Automated journalism uses natural language generation (NLG) technology to create text-based content from digitally structured information.[1359] Initial instances of using NLG technology for automated journalism are limited to brief writings in specific topics but yet demonstrate outstanding quality and quantity.[1360] The generated text is nearly identical to that of human writers, and the volume of documents created

---

[1348] Ibid.

[1349] Ibid.

[1350] Ibid., p. 866

[1351] Ibid.

[1352] Ibid.

[1353] Ibid.

[1354] Monti, Matteo. "Automated Journalism and Freedom of Information: Ethical and Juridical Problems Related to AI in the Press Field." *Opinio Juris in Comparatione* 1 (2018): p. 1.

[1355] Ibid.

[1356] Ibid., p. 2

[1357] Ibid.

[1358] Ibid.

[1359] Ibid.

[1360] Ibid.

far exceeds that of manual editorial methods.[1361] Automated journalism involves either writing and publishing news pieces independently or collaborating with a journalist who can provide supervision and feedback.[1362]

The New York Times (*NYT*) pioneered the use of AI in the news office through its 'Editor' initiative, that added social media tags to literary pieces.[1363] *The Washington Post* utilized Heliograf software to cover the 2016 Olympic Games in Rio de Janeiro, collecting data on event schedules, outcomes, and medal tallies.[1364] *WP* now covers financial and local sports news through journalism automation.[1365] *WP* used AI to cover simple local news, reducing expenses and increasing market share and audience.[1366]

Several newer media outlets, including the "Associated Press," *Forbes, Los Angeles Times*, and ProPublica, use journalism automation that relies on structured data for news items.[1367] This strategy offers advantages such as faster data collection and article writing, less errors, and cost savings.[1368] Automated journalism's quality is limited by the data it uses, making it difficult to propose new concerns and conduct in-depth critical examination of the occurrences described.[1369] Current AI articles suffer from poor narrative quality and critical considerations.[1370] The revolution primarily affects media institutions and the rules of professionalism in journalism.[1371] Multimedia organizations are often characterized as having authoritative (regulations processes), moral (also known as the connection between societal ideals and purposes), and cultural-cognitive (the spreading process) characteristics.[1372]

The 'disruptive innovation' of journalism automation has created 'automation anxiety', which is partly unfounded given AI's minimal impact on the media profession.[1373] Fear about technology is unnecessary when used in safe sectors.[1374] To determine the optimal use of automated journalism,

---

[1361] Ibid.
[1362] Ibid.
[1363] Ibid.
[1364] Ibid.
[1365] Ibid.
[1366] Ibid.
[1367] Ibid., p. 3
[1368] Ibid.
[1369] Ibid.
[1370] Ibid., p. 3-4
[1371] Ibid., p.4
[1372] Ibid.
[1373] Ibid., p. 5
[1374] Ibid.

examine the concept of information freedom in the Italian jurisprudence, for example.[1375] The regulation of information freedom varies per legal system globally.[1376] Italy's regulation is well-developed and stated, including active and passive aspects like the right to inform and the right to be informed, similar to those in Europe.[1377]

Case law in the Italian legal system provides specific examples of press freedom and information.[1378] The right to chronicle is the first category in Italian jurisprudence, which involves simply reporting information about a past event.[1379] Journalists have the right to regulate their sources of information, ensuring the authenticity and integrity of their stories.[1380] This includes combining facts with critiques or remarks from the reporter.[1381] The second category in Italian jurisprudence is the right of critique (sometimes called the "right" to criticize), and refers to having the right to criticize a concept, a situation, or other components of democracy.[1382] For legal uses, this privilege necessitates only modest consideration to the veracity of the events being remarked on and analyzed.[1383] The right to critique might be viewed as a type of politically motivated leaflet created by a reporter.[1384] The third category in Italian jurisprudence includes journalistic investigation, which reflects the Press's duty as an enforcer of society.[1385] It comprises of disclosing hypotheses concerning unverified details.[1386] There is less need to check the sources of information.[1387] Automated journalism has the potential to improve news quality and is worth chronicling.[1388] Indeed, in this context, automated journalism could serve as a means for enhancing and giving the right to chronicle more unbiased by gathering and reporting information sans human intervention or manipulation.[1389] This may be the 'purest' or ideal version of the right to chronicle.[1390] This system could benefit from adding information on ancestral histories from government registers along with additional resources.[1391] Instances of applying the right of chronicle include the *Los Angeles Times'*

[1375] Ibid.
[1376] Ibid.
[1377] Ibid.
[1378] Ibid., p. 5-6
[1379] Ibid.
[1380] Ibid.
[1381] Ibid.
[1382] Ibid.
[1383] Ibid.
[1384] Ibid.
[1385] Ibid.
[1386] Ibid.
[1387] Ibid.
[1388] Ibid.
[1389] Ibid.
[1390] Ibid.
[1391] Ibid.

QuakeBot for the reporting of earthquakes and "AP's" Wordsmith platform for corporate earnings reports.[1392] Narration can be challenging when dealing with certain data items.[1393] In some cases, Wordsmith software may be insufficient for reporting on local government activities.[1394]

Therefore, automated journalism appears to be now limited to right-wing chronicle reporting, as software and technology are not developed enough to improve or replace a human's critique.[1395] Because of those and other restrictions, manual reporting will continue to be the sole feasible approach to delivering highly sophisticated, significant, and useful news throughout the time being.[1396] However, it is conceivable to record numerous journalism incidents and narratives into information, automating the creation of information which can be more complicated than typical athletic and financial coverage.[1397] Currently, robot journalism is only used for predictable circumstances.[1398] Automated journalism may uncover new relationships in data, but it cannot explain their causes or implications.[1399] While human thinking is still important for incorrectness of chronicle reporting, AI can provide critique with additional capabilities like fact-checking political remarks and simulating emotions associated with unfair actions.[1400]

Human journalists are necessary when data mining is not feasible.[1401] Automated journalism can free up journalists from covering simple public events, allowing them to focus on more difficult or critique-worthy news.[1402] Automated journalism is not unbiased since the editor picks which articles to publish.[1403] Bias can be introduced by editors and publishers focusing on specific topics, such as crimes committed by immigrants or financial market issues, in order to criticize immigrants or capitalism.[1404]

From a legal standpoint, the two most pressing challenges involving automated journalism are its legal status and the issue of culpability.[1405] The two subjects are inextricably linked because the

---

[1392] Ibid.
[1393] Ibid.
[1394] Ibid.
[1395] Ibid., p. 7
[1396] Ibid.
[1397] Ibid.
[1398] Ibid.
[1399] Ibid.
[1400] Ibid.
[1401] Ibid.
[1402] Ibid.
[1403] Ibid.
[1404] Ibid.
[1405] Ibid., p. 8

problem of AI protection of speech has repercussions for accountability.[1406] Vexing question of algorithmic security is the first issue.[1407] Scholars in the US have questioned whether algorithms' output is protected under the First Amendment.[1408] To summarize the widely supported position, the result of a computation should be deemed speech that is protected if it contains an informative statement.[1409] From this vantage point, algorithm security may appear to be acceptable, however, the communication generated by a computer algorithm may not be considered legal.[1410] "Who wrote this speech?" is the second issue.[1411] On the other hand, and maybe more relevant, "to whom is responsible for the AI-generated speech?"[1412] Actually, it may be feasible to differentiate the individual who speaks or creator of the AI-generated speech with the topic responsible for the utterance.[1413] Following the foregoing, it is possible to argue that the algorithm outputs are considered freedom of speech without human interaction, but responsibility must be defined.[1414] The concept of responsibility is crucial in the realm of AI.[1415] It determines the type of AI, its application, and whether its advantages are shared by everybody.[1416] Liability for AI actions, including imputation and automated journalism, is a major legal issue.[1417]

As previously said, AI has yet to be sophisticated adequately to generate journalism that is critical or choose what to make available.[1418] Therefore, only the initial two kinds of liability theories may be fulfilled.[1419] The term 'perpetration via AI' refers to when an editor or programmer uses AI to make fake news or malign someone, resulting in clear culpability for their actions.[1420] However, if the AI's erroneous or libelous output is the result of developers' or writers' negligence (the 'natural-probable consequence liability model'), the problem appears to be more problematic and relates to the necessity of the adoption of some due diligence standard.[1421] When the absence of an actual human author moves accountability over to the editor-in-chief, like in the instance of an anonymous piece,

---

[1406] Ibid.
[1407] Ibid.
[1408] Ibid.
[1409] Ibid.
[1410] Ibid.
[1411] Ibid.
[1412] Ibid.
[1413] Ibid.
[1414] Ibid.
[1415] Ibid.
[1416] Ibid.
[1417] Ibid.
[1418] Ibid., p. 9
[1419] Ibid.
[1420] Ibid.
[1421] Ibid., p. 9-10

were developers or technologists responsible to the AI's results?[1422] Verified sources or editors can analyze particular components that comprise the results, yet they are unable to confirm every aspect of the algorithm itself, let alone the technological method through which the algorithm generates the news.[1423]

Errors in programming can cause the algorithm to overlook pre-determined data, resulting in distorted output.[1424] The editor and fact-checker may not be able to detect this.[1425] Editors and fact checkers may not grasp the algorithm's code; therefore, they rely on programmers and engineers to create effective algorithms.[1426] NLG technology continues to be equivalent to editing tasks requiring computational intelligence than programming.[1427] However, it is still not a prevalent skill set in journalism education. As a result, the programmer's responsibilities cannot be overlooked.[1428]

In automated journalism, programmers should be held accountable for negligence or intentional misconduct.[1429] Legislators or courts should establish or develop certain types of liabilities.[1430] Creating and enforcing laws, including *ad hoc* ones, is a pressing concern.[1431] The absence of *ad hoc* regulations and automated journalism rules raises concerns about data use and ethical issues that media firms may not be able to handle without legislative intervention.[1432]

Scholars and journalists frequently regard ethical best practices and ethical challenges as key variables in analyzing new media technologies in order to better journalistic work.[1433] The benefits of computerized journalism might include enhancements in the constitutional category of the right to chronicle, which happens to be the primary field where neutrality is required.[1434] The employment of algorithms capable of producing an article straight from a set of data could improve the accuracy and objectivity of fact-based news reporting.[1435] Automated journalism is most effective for fact-based

---

[1422] Ibid., p. 10
[1423] Ibid.
[1424] Ibid.
[1425] Ibid.
[1426] Ibid.
[1427] Ibid.
[1428] Ibid.
[1429] Ibid.
[1430] Ibid.
[1431] Ibid.
[1432] Ibid.
[1433] Ibid., p. 11
[1434] Ibid.
[1435] Ibid.

stories using reliable and structured data.[1436] Automated journalism can decrease costs and allow journalists to focus on more important topics, including critiquing reported events and facts.[1437]

However, automated journalism raises many ethical concerns.[1438] Aside from the application of automated journalism for manufacturing disinformation, moral issues surrounding AI's development of headlines may be analyzed.[1439] Current use of AI in article writing increases anxieties on data quality and accuracy.[1440] Problems with this topic include identifying the source of the data, ensuring correctness, and avoiding modification to maintain its integrity.[1441]

The first issue pertains to the identity and transparency of data sources.[1442] In fact, this may be morally beneficial to inform audiences about the information resources utilized by AI to generate an article.[1443] Utilizing information collected by a 'political' resource as well as an impartial/public agency may be appropriate, regardless of the criteria utilized to obtain the data differ between a political actor and an independent one.[1444] The most crucial factor is that the reader understands the origin of the dataset used by AI.[1445] It is vital to note that AI databases can be accessible to everyone, freely available, or require a request for access.[1446] Additionally, data use may be illegal.[1447] Utilizing this terminology, the information's source may be equivalent to the informant's identification.[1448] Nevertheless, in accordance with the concept of honesty, considering the possibility of AI harm, the information's source ought to constantly be disclosed.[1449] Being open regarding a dataset's provenance could render identifying the 'informant identity' for the information (as well as the chink within its safety framework) simpler, yet the responsibility for the information circulated appears to grow of greater significance in so far that it tells the general discussion as well as the political discussion of information, as well as the dangers of neglect in AI reporting have been significant in terms of disinformation and deception.[1450] Additionally, it is indisputable that genuine data may

---

[1436] Ibid.
[1437] Ibid.
[1438] Ibid.
[1439] Ibid.
[1440] Ibid.
[1441] Ibid.
[1442] Ibid., p. 12
[1443] Ibid.
[1444] Ibid.
[1445] Ibid.
[1446] Ibid.
[1447] Ibid.
[1448] Ibid.
[1449] Ibid.
[1450] Ibid.

originate via a purely political origin.[1451] Ethically, customers have a duty to understand the data sources utilized in automated reporting, just as they have the right to know a newspaper's political perspective.[1452]

The second concern is the 'quality' of the data used to construct the article (i.e., accuracy and correctness).[1453] Algorithms eliminate typos and arithmetic errors, leading to a lower mistake rate.[1454] Most errors are caused by an issue with the data.[1455] Poor data tells a negative story.[1456] To address this issue, it is ethical to use only correct, objective, and accurate data.[1457] Automation is most effective in fields like banking, sports, and weather where data suppliers provide accuracy and reliability.[1458] Without to mention, computerization is unable to be used in areas where there is no accessible data.[1459] Automation is difficult in cases where the data quality is low.[1460] When selecting a dataset, it is important to prioritize accuracy and reliability, especially if the source is political.[1461] Imagine an information set created by a firm or compiled by a group of politicians.[1462] Such resources may also be utilized if they happen to be 'politically' focused, yet irrespective of the fact that they only gather the information they desire or require (for example, gathering only the arrest histories of immigrants, the benefits of product marketing, or aptitude test findings from a parochial school), the reliability of the information should be guaranteed.[1463] The developer, writer, or editor has to verify the data's accuracy and authenticity.[1464] Verification is also required for datasets handled by public authorities.[1465]

Using unreliable data can lead to fake news (e.g., *The Los Angeles Times's* Quakebot reporting of an inexistent earthquake) and financial reports that are inaccurate (e.g., Netflix's second-quarter earnings error in 2015).[1466] Browsing for correct information and cross-checking multiple databases

---

[1451] Ibid.
[1452] Ibid.
[1453] Ibid.
[1454] Ibid.
[1455] Ibid.
[1456] Ibid.
[1457] Ibid.
[1458] Ibid., p. 12-13
[1459] Ibid., p.13
[1460] Ibid.
[1461] Ibid.
[1462] Ibid.
[1463] Ibid.
[1464] Ibid.
[1465] Ibid.
[1466] Ibid.

might prevent embarrassing mistakes and fake news.[1467]

In addition, robotic journalism may only be employed if the information is reliable and foreseeable occurrences; nonetheless, a moral duty ought to exist to oversee the procedure of developing and disseminating automated journalism content.[1468] This brings us to the final moral premise which ought to act as the foundation for computerized reporting: Supervision via an independent researcher as well as a writer may help prevent the unavoidable mistakes that machines commit.[1469] Perhaps, the greatest detrimental elements of automated journalism is the lack of product monitoring and validation.[1470] Dedicated surveillance and validation may avoid or reduce mistakes caused by, say, unexpected occurrences or deceptive information.[1471] The two most typical faults in this type of ML are named after mathematicians: Type I (false negative) and Type II (false positive).[1472] A proofreading method for AI-generated content ought to be made necessary in the media area, allowing fact-checkers and editors to be held accountable for negligence.[1473] The fourth ethical issue is data distortion caused by ill faith or bias in AI algorithms.[1474] This first component has already been addressed in journalism ethics: creating fake news and distorting facts and data is illegal.[1475] As a result, the remedy is simple and obvious: prohibit such behavior.[1476] The second component is revolutionary, as AI bias might affect data reading and news story accuracy.[1477]

Journalists can utilize data, computers, and algorithms in the public interest, but it is important to consider how, when, where, why, and who.[1478] While automated journalism has the potential to enhance news quality and accuracy, some ethical and legal guidelines must be created.[1479] Enshrining moral values within an agreement of behavior can help courts apply current statutes, interpret them for AI, and follow good practices throughout liability cases.[1480]

To address liability concerns, editors can design methods to check automated journalism

---

[1467] Ibid.
[1468] Ibid.
[1469] Ibid.
[1470] Ibid.
[1471] Ibid.
[1472] Ibid., p.13-14
[1473] Ibid., p.14
[1474] Ibid.
[1475] Ibid.
[1476] Ibid.
[1477] Ibid.
[1478] Ibid, p. 16
[1479] Ibid.
[1480] Ibid.

results.[1481] To minimize liability in a defamation case, organizations can implement monitoring processes or verify data sources.[1482] Implementing criminal and civil liability for automated journalism can ensure accuracy by monitoring and fact-checking algorithm outputs.[1483] This is the most straightforward approach to ensuring ethical norms are followed, as long as the 'offenses' can be verified by a non-programmer.[1484] *Ad hoc* legislation may be required to delegate accountability to developers.[1485]

Considering the inherent political aspect of selecting which news stories to release, robotic journalism poses several questions concerning the foreseeable future of the media, most notably ethical concerns.[1486] The biggest issues stem from data usage, which can be addressed through best practices and liability laws.[1487] The aforementioned ethical standards might thus be established with a code of conduct that would be imposed on personnel participating with novel journalistic technology and, ideally, coupled to creative law governing programmers' liability.[1488] Obviously, a kind of autonomy for the group of techno-journalists would be preferable as a supplement.[1489] To summarize, given these guidelines, automated journalism may provide benefits to the field of media, but it cannot replace journalists.[1490] Humans are going to keep playing an essential part in journalism since the type of criticism required for comprehending the information is unable to be accomplished by an automated system.[1491] There is no AI device that at present hold authorities responsible for their decisions.[1492] A robot journalist cannot be a protector of democracy and human rights.[1493] Journalists must comprehend and adapt to changes in their profession to maintain and strengthen their vital social role.[1494]

[1481] Ibid.

[1482] Ibid.

[1483] Ibid., p.16-17

[1484] Ibid., p. 17

[1485] Ibid.

[1486] Ibid.

[1487] Ibid.

[1488] Ibid.

[1489] Ibid.

[1490] Ibid.

[1491] Ibid.

[1492] Ibid.

[1493] Ibid.

[1494] Ibid.

7 AI AND REAL ESTATE

According to Kasyanau (2024), before technological advancements, the real estate market was primarily reliant on human operations.[1495] Agents and brokers maintained substantial personal networks, conducting business primarily through word-of-mouth referrals and tangible property listings.[1496] Property and lead searches were both time-consuming tasks.[1497] The dramatic distinction among the pre-tech real estate industry and today's AI-driven one demonstrates the revolutionary power of innovation.[1498] This has transformed the entire sector, from property searches and inspections to client interactions and market forecasting.[1499]

According to Lecko (2024), the appraisal of property has been an important part of the real estate market.[1500] Appraisal affects both consumer decisions and the investor to buy, sell, and renovate.[1501] Previously, property appraisals were calculated by manually comparing recent market data.[1502] Companies like Zillow, for example, would collect large quantities of information and utilize it to generate estimates.[1503] However, the advent of AI has improved creativity and novel instruments to this procedure.[1504] To do the aforementioned, inventors used ML along with other AI technologies

---

[1495] Kasyanau, Andrei. "How Artificial Intelligence Is Changing the Real Estate Market." Forbes, October 30, 2024. https://www.forbes.com/councils/forbestechcouncil/2024/10/30/how-artificial-intelligence-is-changing-the-real-estate-market/.

[1496] Ibid.
[1497] Ibid.
[1498] Ibid.
[1499] Ibid.
[1500] Lecko, David. "The Complete Guide to AI in Real Estate." DealMachine, October 1, 2024. https://www.dealmachine.com/blog/ai-real-estate.

[1501] Ibid.
[1502] Ibid.
[1503] Ibid.
[1504] Ibid.

to deliver precise property value and price.[1505] Such innovative AI-powered home appraisal and valuation systems leverage massive quantities of information with advanced codes to deliver accurate and predicted assessments for house repairs.[1506] As opposed to making straightforward contrasts, these methods employ a wide assortment of factors, such as home qualities, geographic characteristics, historic property values, upward trends in prices, community statistics, and socioeconomic factors.[1507] These valuation systems also rely heavily on ML.[1508] For instance, entrepreneurs may develop algorithms on historical information to determine how precise their appraisal methods work.[1509] To take it one level more, once taught and examined, such prognostic assessments may detect hidden characteristics which people are unlikely to discover or even be aware of.[1510] These invisible characteristics help AI-powered home appraisal tools produce incredibly precise appraisals and progressively smart value suggestions.[1511]

Traditionally, looking for a property has been a time-consuming and laborious process.[1512] Nevertheless, the development of AI networks has made home searches more efficient and customized.[1513] As a consequence, every person's job in the marketplace for real estate is increasingly organized and productive.[1514] A few primary explanations why the AI-driven search for properties is successful was its capacity to acquire knowledge from its consumers.[1515] For instance, whenever a prospective purchaser utilizes the platform to look for a house, the individual using it provides both direct and indirect feedback based on their behavior.[1516] Participation directly may involve completing a form on the website, ranking the suggestions with a thumbs up or down, and so on.[1517] Users can provide indirect feedback through posting a home hyperlink, activating buttons, taking a long time seeing a property, contrasting it to other properties, and so on.[1518]

After examining every piece of information collected through different user activities, AI may assess whether or not the purchasing encounter was good or bad, effective or ineffective, and, lastly,

---

[1505] Ibid.
[1506] Ibid.
[1507] Ibid.
[1508] Ibid.
[1509] Ibid.
[1510] Ibid.
[1511] Ibid.
[1512] Ibid.
[1513] Ibid.
[1514] Ibid.
[1515] Ibid.
[1516] Ibid.
[1517] Ibid.
[1518] Ibid.

whether an agreement to buy occurred.[1519] Given the results of the review, AI can experiment with fresh changes regarding its suggestion engine.[1520] Although these modifications could render the device somewhat imperfect in the near future, they eventually lead to more accurate and matched suggestions across an array of purchasers.[1521] Customization allows these algorithms to make more specific recommendations.[1522] Using data points provided by a customer, algorithms may improve their offerings according to previous customer habits and past purchases in a certain location.[1523] Based on data AI is particularly effective in personalized shopping experiences for consumers.[1524]

Digital property has evolved into a convenient manner to see properties for sale.[1525] AI algorithms allow digital real estate search portals to offer potential purchasers genuine experiences in virtual reality.[1526] Such websites provide purchasers a comprehensive approach to browse the market for real estate, moving beyond facts and figures found in internet searches.[1527] Intelligent AI can construct interactive tours and models which give the impression of actually being present by combining massive quantities of information, models in three dimensions, videos, pictures, and AR.[1528] The primary benefit of a virtual residence discovery is that it saves prospective house buyers time and effort.[1529] Consumers are no longer needed to visit five or ten homes because they can narrow their options by electronically viewing them.[1530] Input from an online home visit may be applied to the previously stated improved home exploration.[1531] Greater encounters, comments, and information equals satisfied homebuyers.[1532]

In the vast, chaotic, and fierce environment of housing markets, effective marketing strategies are critical for profitability.[1533] Property engagement software is transforming the way agents identify and contact prospective buyers.[1534] These approaches are revolutionary for property marketing.[1535]

[1519] Ibid.
[1520] Ibid.
[1521] Ibid.
[1522] Ibid.
[1523] Ibid.
[1524] Ibid.
[1525] Ibid.
[1526] Ibid.
[1527] Ibid.
[1528] Ibid.
[1529] Ibid.
[1530] Ibid.
[1531] Ibid.
[1532] Ibid.
[1533] Ibid.
[1534] Ibid.
[1535] Ibid.

Over the near future, shareholders could anticipate further AI interfaces utilizing this form of technology, which will keep working to enhance the experience for users.[1536] Some of the primary advantages of intelligent real estate marketing includes the computerization of promotional activities.[1537] Resources-consuming processes such as prospect creation, nurturing leads, and subsequent interactions can be computerized, freeing up realtors' time to focus on the essential elements of their organization.[1538] DealMachine, for instance, offers an automated marketing technology for automation that allows realtors to distribute customized direct mail marketing to homeowners and following up automatically.[1539] Automated methods such as those may spare significant amount of energy and anxiety.[1540] A user can just send his or her email, then sit back and relax![1541] The user can rest assured that possible deals will not fall between the gaps owing to mistakes made by humans.[1542]

A further significant advantage is the vast volume of information rendered accessible by sophisticated AI tools and organizers.[1543] AI systems may gather, identify, and store high-quality data for later smart reuse.[1544] Customers can use a collection of more than 150 million properties in the US to generate leads for their marketing campaigns.[1545] Personalization options include more than 70 ready-made filters and 700 variables to help customers refine their specific preferences.[1546]

Generative AI influences AI-powered real estate outreach as well.[1547] Like its title implies, this AI produces outcomes according to the user's choices.[1548] In the property sector, it might be utilized to create difficult-to-search contacts.[1549] Similarly, a skip tracking program provides the homeowner's telephone number along with their email address with just a click of an icon.[1550] Information accuracy and saving time may eventually come together in hand.[1551]

[1536] Ibid.
[1537] Ibid.
[1538] Ibid.
[1539] Ibid.
[1540] Ibid.
[1541] Ibid.
[1542] Ibid.
[1543] Ibid.
[1544] Ibid.
[1545] Ibid.
[1546] Ibid.
[1547] Ibid.
[1548] Ibid.
[1549] Ibid.
[1550] Ibid.
[1551] Ibid.

AI-driven representatives, chatbots, and virtual assistants [VAs], emerged as key components of major firms' customer service strategies worldwide.[1552] Chatbots, agents, and virtual assistants are gaining popularity in the real estate sector.[1553] Such smart representatives have the ability to interact between employees and consumers, offer support according to requests, and simplify pathways for operator contact.[1554] The bulk of robots and digital assistants use NLP and ML to reply to user requests.[1555] Typically, bots are designed to answer frequently requested inquiries.[1556] In other cases, however, they can respond to various queries, similar to ChatGPT.[1557] Online representatives in real estate supplied home details, booked home tours, offered suggestions to consumers, and occasionally handled genuine documentation and agreements.[1558] The key point of focus here is operational efficiency.[1559] If a realtor who does not have to arrange a meeting with everyone who visits his or her website, he or she saves a lot of time and money.[1560]

Forecasting, according to Rossini (2000), is a major difficulty in almost every facet of real estate practice.[1561] Appraisal and valuation are prediction techniques.[1562] The acquisition of property relies on anticipating predicted expenses and profits.[1563] Asset and facility professionals rely on demand and availability estimates, expenses, and profits.[1564] Banks and investment professionals depend on current and projected valuation projections determined by economic development and operations.[1565] Despite their emphasis on prediction, AI and ES are used mainly for bulk assessments.[1566] Yet, looking more closely at the use cases indicates that they are more akin to traditional programming systems.[1567] Early attempts at "automating" or "computer assisting" appraisal date back to the late 1970s, when adequate processing power was available.[1568] Expert systems and AI solutions for residential appraisal have been proposed for more than a decade.[1569]

[1552] Ibid.
[1553] Ibid.
[1554] Ibid.
[1555] Ibid.
[1556] Ibid.
[1557] Ibid.
[1558] Ibid.
[1559] Ibid.
[1560] Ibid.
[1561] Rossini, Peter. "Using expert systems and artificial intelligence for real estate forecasting." In *Sixth Annual Pacific-Rim Real Estate Society Conference, Sydney, Australia*, p. 3. 2000.
[1562] Ibid.
[1563] Ibid.
[1564] Ibid.
[1565] Ibid.
[1566] Ibid.
[1567] Ibid.
[1568] Ibid.
[1569] Ibid.

Rule-based reasoning, case-based reasoning, and neural networks are all proposed ways to mass appraisal and, to a lesser extent, value in general.[1570] Overall, the focus was placed on extracting information from a big property transaction collection.[1571] In other areas of property, the use of AI via neural networks has received less attention.[1572] Deep neural networks have been shown to have proved helpful when calculating a hedonic index of price focused on longitudinal transaction information, although not as effective for data from time series (e.g., average prices).[1573] Other neural network uses include models for residential development demand and cost estimation.[1574]

According to Puttaparthi (2025), real estate organizations frequently face a shortage of workers experienced in AI technology.[1575] To enable easy adoption of AI, overcoming such deficiencies via effective instruction is critical, allowing organizations to completely harness AI's abilities.[1576]

[1570] Ibid.

[1571] Ibid.

[1572] Ibid.

[1573] Ibid.

[1574] Ibid.

[1575] Puttaparthi, Murali. "AI in Real Estate: Use Cases, Challenges, and Future Outlook." AblyPro, 2025. https://ablypro.com/ai-in-real-estate.

[1576] Ibid.

8 ROBO-CHURCH

Since I envisioned this book to be secular non-fiction, I am not allowed to push religion on anyone. This chapter will focus solely on Christianity and I can give opinions that I have faced or gathered, the best that I can legally say it. The next chapter will cover other religions. If you are offended by Christianity, please feel free to skip to the next chapter. One of the requirements for a pastor is to preach the true word of God. AI is created by man, not God. AI materials regarding Christianity are works of the Devil because the Bible did not grant AI permission to preach God's word. AI will misinterpret scripture. There is no such true thing as robo-church. John 14:6 in the King James Version of the Bible states that "Jesus saith unto him, I am the way, the truth, and the life: no man cometh unto the Father, but by me." In other words, accepting Jesus Christ as Lord and Savior is the sole ticket to Heaven, not reliance on technology. For those who do not accept Jesus Christ will go to Hell. Robo-church is indeed "false teaching" away from biblical truth.

Puzio (2023) combines philosophical and religious viewpoints to explore if robots are able to perform purposes related to religion.[1577] The subject of whether robots have rights is central to the field of robot ethics.[1578] The religious perspective adds significant value to robotics.[1579] The emergence of religious robots creates novel moral problems which transcend outside traditional ethics for robots and warrant additional consideration.[1580] This highlights the importance of discussing religious robot ethics.[1581]

[1577] Puzio, Anna. "Robot, Let Us Pray! Can and Should Robots Have Religious Functions? An Ethical Exploration of Religious Robots." *AI & Society* 40, no. 2 (December 11, 2023): p. 1019. https://doi.org/10.1007/s00146-023-01812-z.

[1578] Ibid.
[1579] Ibid.
[1580] Ibid.
[1581] Ibid.

The scientific study of religious beliefs is referred to as theology.[1582] "Robot theology" is the religious study of robotics, including delivery, the Armed Forces, sexual, community, and spiritual robots.[1583] Robots may be studied from various angles, spanning moral, moral-theological, cultural, philosophical, Scriptural, pastoral-theological, educational, and didactic.[1584] The topics covered range from religious philosophy to canon law, providing a thorough overview of this interdisciplinary discipline.[1585] Robot theology encompasses a wide range of subjects, including studies of the body-mind relationship and scriptural investigations into partnerships of alien beings.[1586] It additionally discusses moral issues surrounding the building of communal computers and provides pastoral-theological and normative legal regulations for spiritual robots.[1587]

Religious robots are used to perform religious rites and accompany prayers.[1588] Religious robots, as well as social robots developed for social interactions, can execute religious practices.[1589] These robots discuss religious issues or have religious symbolism.[1590]

Religion offers a unique opportunity for interacting in robots for numerous reasons.[1591] Theology offers numerous examples of partnerships with alien beings, including creatures and hybrid beings in the Bible.[1592] Theology contains moral principles for dealing with others, such as philanthropy and consideration for the marginalized, which addresses both human and religious requirements.[1593] This renders it applicable across societal and theological robots.[1594]

In addition, the technologization process poses significant cultural and moral concerns regarding the perception of humans and the global community.[1595] Technological advancements challenge traditional beliefs about mankind, technology, metaphysics, and the separation of culture and nature, as well as nature and technology.[1596] As a consequence, humanity is grappling over basic concerns

---

[1582] Ibid., p. 1020
[1583] Ibid.
[1584] Ibid.
[1585] Ibid.
[1586] Ibid.
[1587] Ibid.
[1588] Ibid.
[1589] Ibid.
[1590] Ibid.
[1591] Ibid.
[1592] Ibid., p. 1020-1021
[1593] Ibid., p. 1021
[1594] Ibid.
[1595] Ibid.
[1596] Ibid.

like what exactly distinguishes people from devices, concepts of fairness or happiness, or moral use of robotics.[1597] Religion provides a diverse set of responses to ethnographic and moral issues related to humanity and the outside world.[1598] Yet, technological advancements necessitate a new perspective.[1599] Throughout history, humanity have struggled to define their identity in the face of technological advancements.[1600]

Religious themes such as salvation, paradise, omnipotence, relieving suffering, and creation frequently occur in discussions about technology.[1601] The incorporation of religious themes in technology necessitates investigation from a theological perspective.[1602] Religion and robotics are intimately related. Religion may improve the debate on robotics by highlighting its importance.[1603]

There may be issues to robots doing religious practices.[1604] The following outlines two common arguments and their associated concerns.[1605] These concerns might not fully negate the contentions, yet they require rethinking in religious robotic context.[1606]

A major worry involves the fact that robots do not have basic personality traits such as consciousness, intelligence, sentience, and free choice.[1607] Religious practices are typically associated with human-like characteristics.[1608] This objection can be offered in response to the "can" question, implying whether machines might be unable to perform prayers because of their absence of awareness and consciousness.[1609] It illustrates the interconnectedness of the "can" and "should" questions.[1610] Certain actions have traditionally been linked with human agents and properties.[1611] However, technology may now take over some of these activities.[1612]

This criticism is strongly related to the so-called "properties approach," which wields

---

[1597] Ibid.
[1598] Ibid.
[1599] Ibid.
[1600] Ibid.
[1601] Ibid.
[1602] Ibid.
[1603] Ibid.
[1604] Ibid., p. 1023
[1605] Ibid.
[1606] Ibid.
[1607] Ibid.
[1608] Ibid.
[1609] Ibid.
[1610] Ibid.
[1611] Ibid.
[1612] Ibid.

considerable influence within the robotics ethics field.[1613] According to the "properties approach," a robot's moral status is determined by whether it exhibits humanlike characteristics.[1614] This implies how we interact alongside a being, if it has liberties, and if it can act morally, is decided by if it contains characteristics like awareness, mental abilities, intellect, or sentience—which all have historically been associated with humanity alone.[1615] However, the attributes approach has some challenges.[1616] One major obstacle is the complexity of defining these features.[1617] There is still no clear definition of consciousness, despite decades of intellectual inquiry.[1618] People's perceptions of consciousness vary greatly.[1619] Other properties face similar challenges.[1620] The reason "why you cannot make a computer that feels pain" is "nothing to do with the technical challenges of making pain computable." Another issue is "the other minds problem."[1621] A lot of these features represent mental states of consciousness, making it difficult to ascribe them to any creature or thing.[1622] We cannot understand what it is like to be someone else, feel their suffering, or create their experiences.[1623] Determining consciousness or sentience in different entities, such as humans, animals, or robots, becomes more challenging.[1624] Identifying the most important property or group of properties can be tough.[1625]

Many ethical theories advocate for relational approaches as an answer to approaches like the characteristics method used in robotic bioethics.[1626] They underline how we interact to nonhuman creatures, including animals or robots, are shaped by our connections rather than their fundamental features.[1627] While it may appear logical to establish morals upon characteristics inside the moral custom, numerous ways call into inquiry if the everyday life, daily behaviors were truly founded on them.[1628] Interactions with robots have a profound impact on our behavior, making ethical considerations for religious robots crucial.[1629] This is significant as with spiritual robots, the myriad individual and eternal issues implicated can swiftly give rise to a strained connection to the

---

[1613] Ibid., p. 1024
[1614] Ibid.
[1615] Ibid.
[1616] Ibid.
[1617] Ibid.
[1618] Ibid.
[1619] Ibid.
[1620] Ibid.
[1621] Ibid.
[1622] Ibid.
[1623] Ibid.
[1624] Ibid.
[1625] Ibid.
[1626] Ibid.
[1627] Ibid.
[1628] Ibid.
[1629] Ibid.

robot.[1630]

Surprisingly, the lack of awareness and mind may enable more personal and intimate conversations with robots.[1631] Individuals may feel more comfortable confiding in robots, as they believe they can express themselves freely, especially when addressing personal concerns.[1632] The fear barrier is smaller than while discussing personal concerns with a spiritual leader.[1633] Jason Rohrer created Project December in 2020, a website which allowed people to interact with customizable chatbots like Samantha, according to GPT-3 and with their own personalities.[1634] The endeavor received traction after Joshua Barbeau, one of the users, gave the GPT-3 bot messages from his late fiancée Jessica, allowing him to talk with her posthumously.[1635] This conversation provided him with comfort and helped him cope with his grief.[1636]

The second important objection is that religious robots face criticism for lacking religious experiences.[1637] Religious rituals require a human with true experiences to share their encounters and form a special relationship with the divine.[1638] Critics argue that robots perform religious activities superficially and lack authenticity.[1639] Personal experiences are intuitively important in particular settings.[1640] Although valid, this objection raises various concerns.[1641]

Although it is unclear if robots can have religious experiences, it is likely that they will interact with humans.[1642] Robots interact differently than humans due to their unique ways of interpreting and interacting with the world.[1643] This new robotic experience may be beneficial for certain religious practices, despite its differences from human experiences.[1644] Robots' ability to recall information, recognize subtleties in human interactions, and transcend physical limitations may provide valuable insights.[1645]

[1630] Ibid.
[1631] Ibid.
[1632] Ibid.
[1633] Ibid.
[1634] Ibid.
[1635] Ibid.
[1636] Ibid.
[1637] Ibid.
[1638] Ibid., p. 1024-1025
[1639] Ibid., p. 1025
[1640] Ibid.
[1641] Ibid.
[1642] Ibid.
[1643] Ibid.
[1644] Ibid.
[1645] Ibid.

According to Litvinova and Manenkov (2025), a church in Finland displayed avatars of deceased church pastors reading from the Old Testament of the Bible on a huge screen in the sanctuary.[1646] The screen also showed an AI-generated Jesus Christ dressed in garments with long hair.[1647] It also showed an AI-generated Satan dressed in modern clothing, with a frightening frown and a higher-pitched voice.[1648] It was Finland's first church service organized primarily by AI tools, which wrote the sermons and some of the hymns, composed the music, and created the graphics.[1649]

The heavily announced trial service gathered more than 120 people to the church in northeastern Helsinki, well beyond the average weekday attendance.[1650] People arrived from out of town, as did a few foreigners who claimed they did not know Finnish well enough to grasp everything.[1651] The clergy and attendees both loved it, but agreed that technology would not replace human-led services any time soon.[1652]

DeLuca (2024) describes how a pastor from Long Island, New York, used ChatGPT to prepare a church service which comprised an invitation to worship, invocation, pastoral prayer, reading from scripture, message, songs, prelude, postlude, and benediction.[1653] When word of Trump's assassination attempt broke, the pastor felt compelled to amend the previously prepared AI service by requesting that ChatGPT write a church prayer in response to the previous day's tragedy.[1654] He was satisfied with the findings.[1655] Surprisingly, attendance was high.[1656] He has already addressed other sensitive preaching subjects, like comparing Barbie and Ken dolls to Adam and Eve in the book of Genesis of the Bible.[1657]

According to Reed (2022), Tesla has released the first iteration of the humanoid robots, called

---

[1646] Litvinova, Dasha, and Kostya Manenkov. "What One Finnish Church Learned from Creating a Service Almost Entirely with AI." AP News, March 8, 2025. https://apnews.com/article/finland-lutheran-church-artificial-intelligence-64135cc5e58578a89dcbaf0c227d9e3e.

[1647] Ibid.
[1648] Ibid.
[1649] Ibid.
[1650] Ibid.
[1651] Ibid.
[1652] Ibid.
[1653] DeLuca, Renee. "Artificial Intelligence in the Pulpit: A Church Service Written Entirely by AI." United Church of Christ, July 16, 2024. https://www.ucc.org/artificial-intelligence-in-the-pulpit-a-church-service-written-entirely-by-ai/.

[1654] Ibid.
[1655] Ibid.
[1656] Ibid.
[1657] Ibid.

Optimus.[1658] They can simply be called "humanoids."[1659] They have traditionally been used in churches.[1660] A humanoid may be placed in the church lobby to have everyone shaking hands and handing out bulletins.[1661] Similar to church entryway kiosks, the humanoid can sign up for small groups or membership using online forms.[1662] The humanoid might also stroll around, asking parishioners to tithe using Apple Pay.[1663]

Tesla's humanoid robot might be too terrifying as a church greeter.[1664] Even so, they may "volunteer" for something else on a Sunday morning, such as a security detail for the pastor following worship.[1665] Assume someone is chatting for too long, and the line is backing up.[1666] In that situation, the humanoid can assist them, preferably by gently moving them away from the pastor.[1667]

What happens if a humanoid takes over the church's information technology (IT) department?[1668] It could fix the church's WIFI and ensure that the internet is operational in order to broadcast all of those online church services.[1669] Indeed, a robot should be able to communicate with technology more effectively than humans can, align all of those bytes, and ensure that no data packets are dropped.[1670] The humanoid robot gift requires running a church's human relations department.[1671] Every conversation with a humanoid friend can be reported upstream to anyone who is attending church.[1672] The humanoid can automatically examine all social media profiles for misbehavior.[1673] ML allows the humanoid to predict problems before they occur.[1674]

According to Wibowo and Budiono (2024), posthumanism enables people to engage alongside

---

[1658] Reed, Jeff. "4 Ways Your Church Can Use Tesla's New Humanoid Robot." Exponential, November 28, 2022. https://exponential.org/4-ways-your-church-can-use-teslas-new-humanoid-robot/.

[1659] Ibid.
[1660] Ibid.
[1661] Ibid.
[1662] Ibid.
[1663] Ibid.
[1664] Ibid.
[1665] Ibid.
[1666] Ibid.
[1667] Ibid.
[1668] Ibid.
[1669] Ibid.
[1670] Ibid.
[1671] Ibid.
[1672] Ibid.
[1673] Ibid.
[1674] Ibid.

robots that are humanoid.[1675] The development of robots with humanoids is moving quickly.[1676] Into future generations, churches will undoubtedly interface with robotic individuals.[1677] The church has a complex connection with humanoid robots.[1678] Nevertheless, it is apparent that in the posthumanist era, churches must find new ways of understanding and connecting to nonhuman creatures.[1679] Posthumanism dates back to the early 1900s, although its popularity has grown in recent decades.[1680] This is owing, partially, for the increased advancement of AI and robots.[1681] When machines get smarter, it poses philosophical issues about the essence of mankind.[1682]

As AI progresses, humanoid robots will increasingly replace humans for mechanical activities and other roles.[1683] Churches should assess the essential ideals of their faith and if the usage of humanoid robots is consistent with their values and beliefs.[1684] Humanoid robots in the classroom have the potential to aid instructors in learning.[1685] The debate then shifts to the way humanoid machines may connect with the idea of mankind, faith, or the part that they play in religion.[1686] The church must evaluate whether the inclusion of humanoid robots may alter the religious atmosphere and people's religious experiences.[1687] Humanoid robot development must be approached with caution and ethical thought.[1688] Religious organizations have to evaluate the implications of deploying robotic devices for ministry, making ethical choices, and safeguarding the confidentiality of parishioners.[1689] With response with humanoid robot creation, congregations have to stick to their religion's essential values while taking into account the technology's benefits, implications, and ethical ramifications.[1690]

The school of philosophy that challenges the belief that human beings are the sole or more significant type of existence is referred to as posthumanism.[1691] Posthumanists think that

---

[1675] Wibowo, Gandi, and Stephanas Budiono. "The Relationship between the Church and Humanoid Robots in the Posthumanism Era." *KnE Social Sciences*, August 9, 2024, p. 265. https://doi.org/10.18502/kss.v9i22.16726.

[1676] Ibid.
[1677] Ibid.
[1678] Ibid.
[1679] Ibid.
[1680] Ibid.
[1681] Ibid.
[1682] Ibid.
[1683] Ibid., p. 266
[1684] Ibid.
[1685] Ibid.
[1686] Ibid.
[1687] Ibid.
[1688] Ibid.
[1689] Ibid.
[1690] Ibid.
[1691] Ibid.

people constitute a component of a broader structure that includes creatures, devices, and nature.[1692] The religious community has long been viewed as a champion of each person's worth and worthiness.[1693] During posthumanism, churches must adapt to better comprehend and relate to humanoid robots.[1694]

Posthumanism rejects the idea that mankind are the only or greatest aspect of existence, instead emphasizing on the interconnectedness of all species, especially creatures, robots, and nature.[1695] Posthumanism questions traditional notions of humanity, admitting its deficiency in portraying today's complicated reality.[1696] Posthumanism has various consequences for how we perceive one another, where we belong in the universe, and our connection with technological advances.[1697] For instance, posthumanism contends that humanity ought not to think of creatures as being inferior to human beings, but rather as fellow beings who share the planet.[1698] This argues that machines should be viewed as potential collaborators in human evolution, rather than just tools.[1699] Posthumanism is a difficult and complex motion, yet is crucial for comprehending our world.[1700] As technology advances, posthumanism will become more crucial in understanding our place in the universe.[1701]

Jambrek (2024) defines "spiritual literacy" as a capacity to see the realm of the spirit, comprehend and analyze heavenly occurrences, and the repercussions of supernatural powers at action on Earth.[1702] "Biblical-spiritual" knowledge represents the capacity to acquire knowledge of the realm of the supernatural as demonstrated through the Bible; to comprehend and analyze religious happenings according to Holy Scripture; to understand the functions of evil entities in modern society; and to successfully utilize all Scriptural tools (such as God's Word and Holy Spirit gifts) for the prudent choice of AI devices, infrastructure, and uses.[1703] Spiritual literacy plays a crucial role in appraising AI technologies, particularly at the second and third tiers of creation, such as artificial general intelligence (AGI) and artificial superintelligence (ASI).[1704] In the second and third tiers of

---

[1692] Ibid.

[1693] Ibid.

[1694] Ibid.

[1695] Ibid.

[1696] Ibid.

[1697] Ibid.

[1698] Ibid, p. 266-267

[1699] Ibid., p. 267

[1700] Ibid.

[1701] Ibid.

[1702] Jambrek, Stanko. "Christians Facing the Challenges of Artificial Intelligence." *Kairos: Evangelical Journal of Theology* 18, no. 1 (2024): p. 85.

[1703] Ibid.

[1704] Ibid.

AI creation, engineers design systems and robots that mimic humans and God (god-like AI).[1705] As with Satan, this interferes with God's creative plan.[1706]

According to Ryan (2024), biblical theology should inform all perspectives on the use (and misuse) of AI technologies.[1707] One of the most significant impediments to gospel progress is the linguistic barrier.[1708] The most recent AI techniques, particularly those developed by groups like OpenAI, could swiftly and precisely interpret text in writing and spoken words into various languages, benefiting both biblical translations and Bible study.[1709] Whisper, OpenAI's automatic voice recognition system, is intended to translate spoken language into written writing in the preferred language of the believer.[1710] Whisper can recognize spoken language and transcribe it into various languages almost simultaneously.[1711] Imagine teaching a Bible study with people from various backgrounds and native languages in attendance.[1712]

Human translators are typically required to bridge the language divide.[1713] However, these new AI tools have the potential to serve as an efficient, personalized translation for each individual in their preferred language.[1714] Microsoft Teams, a real-time collaboration and communication program, now uses AI-enabled technologies to deliver live captions for virtual meetings, including the ability to convert a speaker's words into captions printed in the selected language as they are uttered.[1715] Technologies such as OpenAI and Microsoft Teams offer the ability to making Christian teaching more readily available than before.[1716] New AI capabilities offer an opportunity for making the Bible available in more languages compared to earlier.[1717] The Bible is still unavailable in around 3,700 languages.[1718] One business, Avodah, is pioneering the use of AI to translate scripture faster than ever before.[1719] Translators and linguists may swiftly produce preliminary versions of translated scripture

---

[1705] Ibid.

[1706] Ibid.

[1707] Ryan, Dustin. "A Christian's Perspective on Artificial Intelligence." Christ Over All, May 6, 2024. https://christoverall.com/article/longform/a-christians-perspective-on-artificial-intelligence/.

[1708] Ibid.

[1709] Ibid.

[1710] Ibid.

[1711] Ibid.

[1712] Ibid.

[1713] Ibid.

[1714] Ibid.

[1715] Ibid.

[1716] Ibid.

[1717] Ibid.

[1718] Ibid.

[1719] Ibid.

using breakthrough AI methods such as those developed by Avodah, which can subsequently be vetted and modified by human professionals.[1720] Avodah and other organizations' work has the ability to reach many more people and lead them to believe in the gospel.[1721]

Another example involves churches and their virtual presence.[1722] In this increasingly digital world, most churches have an internet or social media presence.[1723] Churches use the World Wide Web (an increasingly outmoded technology) to communicate events, distribute news and announcements, invite unreached people to Easter Sunday, and spread the Gospel.[1724] AI may be the solution for churches with a small staff but a strong need to communicate through visual art and digital graphics.[1725]

Few small churches have full-time staff with the capacity or professional skills to produce high-quality graphics for Christian outreach.[1726] However, generative AI tools can let an unskilled person rapidly and efficiently create eye-catching drawings and pictures that could be used to invite members of the local community to the church's Christmas Eve service, Wednesday potluck lunch, or nighttime Bible study.[1727] The abilities of AI devices provide a thrilling opportunity to interact as well as reaching across to local neighborhoods sharing the reality of the Good News in ways not seen before.[1728] In this and many other ways, AI has the potential to transform Christian ministry, as well as Christians working in hundreds of other vocations.[1729]

AI tools may be utilized to create fake footage, occasionally referred to as "deepfakes," that are intended to fool and deceive viewers.[1730] A deepfake is a video or audio file in which one person's likeness is replaced with that of another.[1731] Using this method, a malicious person using cutting-edge AI technology could film a person doing and saying potentially shocking things while replacing the original person's likeness with that of an influential political figure, celebrity, or other person with the express purpose of causing harm to their reputation or image.[1732] Deepfake AI technology has gotten

---

[1720] Ibid.
[1721] Ibid.
[1722] Ibid.
[1723] Ibid.
[1724] Ibid.
[1725] Ibid.
[1726] Ibid.
[1727] Ibid.
[1728] Ibid.
[1729] Ibid.
[1730] Ibid.
[1731] Ibid.
[1732] Ibid.

so realistic and lifelike that it is frequently undetectable to the typical individual inexperienced with the technology.[1733]

According to Lucky (2023), the Southern Baptist Convention (SBC) passed a statement on ethics of AI, which stated that "human dignity should be central to any ethical principles, guidelines, or regulations for any and all uses of these powerful emerging technologies."[1734] These suggested standards do not address issues with interface design, push alerts, or emoji usage.[1735] They cannot instruct a Christian developer on why robots ought to disclose the source of their knowledge, which conversational themes ought to be avoided, or just how personal a discussion ought to be permitted to get.[1736] They do give a baseline for Christian technology professionals developing AI for medical, criminal justice, and environmental applications, as well as those developing our chatbot instructors, customer service representatives, and therapists.[1737]

According to Gruchola, Slawek-Czochra, and Ziellinski (2024), AI algorithms have an impact on individual prayer practices.[1738] The Roman Catholic Church recognizes the importance of religion in Polish society, despite ongoing secularization (referred to as "creeping secularization").[1739] AI technology has influenced this aspect of everyday existence.[1740] Furthermore, the rapid expansion of knowledge and communication encourages parishioners to think more closely about AI's ethical and religious implications.[1741]

The modern world, characterized by rapid technical advancement, expansion, and countless societal shifts, presents an unusual obstacle for conventional institutions, notably the Roman Catholic Church.[1742] Human behavior in the age of technology, continuing secularization procedures, and sociocultural development appear to be shaping an entirely novel world in

---

[1733] Ibid.

[1734] Lucky, Kate. "AI Will Shape Your Soul." Christianity Today, October 2023. https://www.christianitytoday.com/2023/09/artificial-intelligence-robots-soul-formation/.

[1735] Ibid.
[1736] Ibid.
[1737] Ibid.

[1738] Gruchoła, Małgorzata, Małgorzata Sławek-Czochra, and Robert Zieliński. "Artificial Intelligence as a Tool Supporting Prayer Practices." Religions 15, no. 3 (February 22, 2024): 271. https://doi.org/10.3390/rel15030271.

[1739] Ibid.
[1740] Ibid.
[1741] Ibid.
[1742] Ibid.

conversation with the teachings of faith.[1743] Roman Catholicism, a prominent spiritual, ethical, and intellectual organization, should adjust to current conditions in order to stay current and successful in appealing to contemporary culture.[1744] Technological advancements have transformed interpersonal communication, impacting how people connect with faith principles and participate in Catholic activities.[1745] Interpersonal communication has evolved dramatically as technology has advanced, altering how people identify with religious beliefs and participate in Church community life.[1746] As the opposite direction, technological advances and virtual forums provide novel opportunities for evangelism and discussion.[1747] However, they make it challenging to create authentic spiritual experiences in the digital environment.[1748] Such issues are consistent to the two different fundamental and operational understandings of faith.[1749] These could result in the attribution of supernatural attributes to AI-driven technologies which perform numerous duties traditionally associated with religion.[1750]

Combining AI and prayer is an intriguing issue that bridges the gap between technology and spirituality.[1751] Before delving into this topic, it is important to explore the necessity of touching the sacred in the spiritual realm.[1752] It is important to consider if AI-based applications convey the profane without infringing on the sacred.[1753] Around the showcase galleries of Paris' Pompidou Center in 2020, AI employed mechanical plastic mouths to perform robotic chants.[1754] An algorithm has been developed to collect and produce a universal prayer, making this conceivable. Starting a new religion may lead to the creation of a messiah or God.[1755]

Calo (2024) suggests that before discussing how Christian ethics can apply to AI in healthcare, it is vital to understand Christian perspectives on AI in general.[1756] Christian ethical perspectives on

---

[1743] Ibid.
[1744] Ibid.
[1745] Ibid.
[1746] Ibid.
[1747] Ibid.
[1748] Ibid.
[1749] Ibid.
[1750] Ibid.
[1751] Ibid.
[1752] Ibid.
[1753] Ibid.
[1754] Ibid.
[1755] Ibid.
[1756] Calo, Zachary R. "AI, Medicine and Christian Ethics." *Research Handbook on Health, AI and the Law*, 2024, p. 220. https://doi.org/10.4337/9781802205657.ch13.

AI and health are mostly based on theological evaluations.[1757] It is often held that Christian theology, and maybe most religious thought in general, is innately resistive to AI.[1758] So, the argument goes, Christianity believes that human nature was created *imago Dei*, in the image of God.[1759] This nature is set and inviolable, as well as unique and special.[1760] Artificially altering or replicating something violates its inherent dignity, which is unique to humans.[1761] Arrogating the Divine prerogative is a pinnacle act of hubris by creatures seeking to become Creators.[1762] Some view enhanced human understanding and control of nature as impious, hubristic, or defying the natural order, while others support it.[1763] Religious thought is often viewed as impious, arrogant, and defying authority.[1764]

According to Kamai (2023), while most theologians may not pay much attention, certain engineers are confident that AI will eventually move toward autonomy.[1765] The distance may or may not be significant, but either way, the trend raises severe concerns for Christianity and other global religions.[1766] By reality, AI could pose the most serious danger to Christianity since Charles Darwin's *On the Origin of Species*.[1767] AI has the potential to self-redesign and evolve at a rapid pace once developed by humans.[1768] Human beings, limited by sluggish evolution of biology, are powerless and will be surpassed.[1769]

The assumption is supported by history, as important scientific advances have often had religious implications.[1770] In the 1600s, Galileo promoted heliocentrism, which called into question traditional Christian readings of Bible scriptures claiming that the earth was at the center of the cosmos.[1771] The notion of natural selection, popularized by Charles Darwin in the 1800s, contradicted conventional

---

[1757] Ibid.
[1758] Ibid.
[1759] Ibid.
[1760] Ibid.
[1761] Ibid.
[1762] Ibid.
[1763] Ibid.
[1764] Ibid.
[1765] Kamai, Peter H. "Artificial Intelligence and the Future of Christianity: A Threat or Potential." *AKU: An African Journal of Contemporary Research* 4, no. 3 (2023): p. 84. https://doi.org/10.13140/RG.2.2.25435.54567 .

[1766] Ibid.
[1767] Ibid.
[1768] Ibid.
[1769] Ibid.
[1770] Ibid.
[1771] Ibid.

Christian views about life's genesis.[1772] The trend has persisted with current genetics and climatology.[1773] The development of autonomous robots has the potential to significantly disrupt religion and other fields.[1774] Creating free-willed entities would require reinterpreting all aspects of orthodox theology.[1775]

Concerns about a new world order developing as a result of AI advancements are growing.[1776] While some religious groups have embraced the concept, others remain concerned about potential consequences.[1777] Some religious groups promote AI as a step toward God's plan, despite concerns about its potential impact on the military and jobs.[1778] Given the exponential rate at which AI is progressing, it is not impossible to imagine an advanced AI reaching awareness and maybe serving as God's messenger to facilitate our lives.[1779] Eliminating AI is a difficult task, similar to removing religion from humans.[1780] Religious organizations use AI, which is profoundly ingrained in our genetics, to promote their views and improve religion practices.[1781] There are various options for tracking daily readings and prayer regimens, including apps, chatbots, and humanoid robots designed for rituals.[1782]

According to Prince (2025), some religious leaders were concerned that the printing press, established in the 1400s to produce the Gutenberg Bible, might threaten religious power.[1783] Once radio was introduced, there had been worries regarding transmitting messages to individuals whom were not actually there.[1784] Every technical innovation caused comparable disputes in religious communities.[1785] AI is extremely useful for the following tasks: discovering data rapidly (such as scriptures on particular subjects), organizing a believer's thoughts when stalled, interpreting materials to make it more accessible, developing visuals or footage for worship services, and outlining lengthy

---

[1772] Ibid.

[1773] Ibid.

[1774] Ibid.

[1775] Ibid., p. 84-85

[1776] Ibid., p. 92

[1777] Ibid.

[1778] Ibid.

[1779] Ibid.

[1780] Ibid.

[1781] Ibid.

[1782] Ibid.

[1783] Prince, Nick. "Can I Use AI as a Christian? Here's How to Use Artificial Intelligence Well." Finds, April 10, 2025. https://finds.life.church/ai-as-a-christian-in-ministry/.

[1784] Ibid.

[1785] Ibid.

documents.[1786] AI cannot establish an intimate connection with Jesus Christ, sense the Holy Spirit's direction, comprehend the profound meaning of one's religious excursion, substitute real prayer or worship, or replace true communion with fellow Christians.[1787] Although AI can assist in disseminating the word, only God can convert people's hearts.[1788]

According to Gonzalez (2024), if God is known as the Creator, humanity should be viewed as the creator of AI.[1789] That is why true spirituality will never be discovered by AI.[1790] Only because of what the Bible says and the believer's relationship with God can others be asked to walk with him.[1791] Love only comes from God, not from a computer algorithm.[1792] Joy comes from God and is the source of peace.[1793] These things can flow through someone who is connected to God.[1794] They cannot originate from a machine.[1795] No software will ever be able to repair a broken soul.[1796] That is something only God can do.[1797]

[1786] Ibid.

[1787] Ibid.

[1788] Ibid.

[1789] Gonzalez, Eliezer. "Artificial Intelligence and Christianity." Good News Unlimited, January 14, 2024. https://goodnewsunlimited.com/artificial-intelligence-and-christianity/.

[1790] Ibid.

[1791] Ibid.

[1792] Ibid.

[1793] Ibid.

[1794] Ibid.

[1795] Ibid.

[1796] Ibid.

[1797] Ibid.

9 AI IN OTHER RELIGIONS

This chapter will cover other religions. Like in the last chapter, if these religions offend you, you can skip to the next chapter.

According to Harris (2017), former Google executive Anthony Levandowski founded the Way of the Future (WOTF), an AI-generated religion.[1798] It was an unusual next step of the California-based technology prodigy in the midst of the high-profiled litigation involving Uber and Waymo, Alphabet's self-driving car firm.[1799] According to documents filed with the Internal Revenue Service (IRS), he was the head (or "Dean") of the new religion and the chief executive officer (CEO) of the nonprofit business founded to manage it.[1800]

In the Waymo-Uber lawsuit, Levandowski was charged with obtaining autonomous vehicle information illegally with an 18-year prison sentence in 2020.[1801] He believed that a change was on the way that would alter every element of life for humans, including job opportunities, relaxation, faith, and finances, and could even determine the human species' fate.[1802]

According to Korosec (2021), Levandowski avoided the prison sentence after Trump pardoned

---

[1798] Harris, Mark. "Inside the First Church of Artificial Intelligence." Wired, November 15, 2017. https://www.wired.com/story/anthony-levandowski-artificial-intelligence-religion/.

[1799] Ibid.

[1800] Ibid.

[1801] Ibid.

[1802] Ibid.

him prior to departing office the first time.[1803] His church was dissolved by the end of 2020.[1804]

Levandowski donated the remaining $172,000 or more to the NAACP Legal Defense Fund after shutting down WOTF, according to Epstein (2024).[1805] In November 2023, however, he proclaimed the revival for the belief, claiming which "couple thousand people" had joined him within a sort of devotion of "things that can see everything, be everywhere, know everything, and maybe help us and guide us in a way that normally you would call God."[1806] In addition, to feed an individual who miraculously avoided imprisonment for stealing and went out wealthy, given the fact that neither of his firms had succeeded in putting autonomous vehicles on the roadways, a little confidence in the existence and kindness of a supernatural appears curiously justified.[1807]

WOTF might represent the initial explicit effort at establishing a religious group on the dread of an infinitely powerful synthetic deity, yet it was neither the biggest nor the most prominent.[1808] A superintelligent computer divinity that is equivalent to Satan and would punish people knew of its potential existence but did not directly contribute to its advancement or development is referred to as Roko's Basilisk.[1809]

According to McBride (2017), robots will be present in all aspects of daily life in the not-too-distant future, from production floors to company headquarters, as well as wars to homes.[1810] Although much research on the societal effects on automation emphasizes ethical concerns such as the financial effect upon human employees or the morality of killing robots, less emphasis is given to the impact of the AI era on faith.[1811] By 2099, AI would most certainly be used in the home as

---

[1803] Korosec, Kirsten. "Anthony Levandowski Closes His Church of AI." TechCrunch, February 18, 2021. https://techcrunch.com/2021/02/18/anthony-levandowski-closes-his-church-of-ai/?guccounter=1&guce_referrer=aHR0cHM6Ly93d3cuYmluZy5jb20v&guce_referrer_sig=AQAAAA7wdmg863gnmTB-zt3TzXLhI2FXY_yVFNL7TZTzFGnraTk6vg36gh2MeUfk6Bbt5qOnfLuRsCKSbhoFhRFjje7PEt--U1yZIAtATNt7MIX9o-Qvlv9Pkrxabs2gOr8gF8z4Bedit26dAJ_GBs2mdbVayvTIp5IJ_bdJ1vX3i69Z.

[1804] Ibid.

[1805] Epstein, Erik. "Silicon Valley's Obsession with AI Looks a Lot like Religion." The MIT Press Reader, November 22, 2024. https://thereader.mitpress.mit.edu/silicon-valleys-obsession-with-ai-looks-a-lot-like-religion/.

[1806] Ibid.
[1807] Ibid.
[1808] Ibid.
[1809] Ibid.
[1810] McBride, James. "Robotic Bodies and the Kairos of Humanoid Theologies." Sophia 58, no. 4 (December 5, 2017): p. 663. https://doi.org/10.1007/s11841-017-0628-3.

[1811] Ibid.

babysitters and caregivers, especially for babies and toddlers.[1812] Parents would like to know what machines will teach their children principles according to their religious heritage.[1813] As a consequence, parents would require AI devices built with proper faith programs, deployed by companies yet authorized by the religious organizations, such as Catholic, Muslim, and Lutheran robots.[1814] When robots develop the ability to reason independently, worshippers would wish to integrate the machines into their faith groups in order to impact the formation of AI religious beliefs.[1815] The Robotic Age will thus pose fundamental religious issues.[1816] It represents an unusual obstacle within the evolution of faith.[1817] While biofundamentalists may oppose radical shifts in religion, a lot of believers may find it hard to reject people who resemble humans in appearance and behavior.[1818]

Jackson, et al. (2023) argue that AI gadgets hold promise for the future of religion, which is declining globally, particularly in East Asia, North America and Europe.[1819] Trustworthy spiritual models who devoted time, wellness, and wealth towards their beliefs may have played a crucial role of sustaining adherents' commitment to religions throughout history.[1820] Historical personalities offer a stark contrast to today's scandal-prone television evangelists and the prospect for robotic preachers in the future.[1821] While it's impossible to predict the future of religion, if religious leaders lose credibility in society, followers may lose faith.[1822]

According to Cockrell (2024), scholars and philosophers have long debated the relationship between science and religion.[1823] Max Weber, a German sociologist, saw science as leading to the "disenchantment of the world," or the replacement of mystical explanations for how the cosmos

---

[1812] Ibid.

[1813] Ibid.

[1814] Ibid.

[1815] Ibid.

[1816] Ibid.

[1817] Ibid.

[1818] Ibid.

[1819] Jackson, Joshua Conrad, Kai Chi Yam, Pok Man Tang, Ting Liu, and Azim Shariff. "Exposure to Robot Preachers Undermines Religious Commitment." *Journal of Experimental Psychology: General* 152, no. 12 (2023): p. 3358. https://doi.org/10.1037/xge0001443.

[1820] Ibid.

[1821] Ibid.

[1822] Ibid.

[1823] Cockrell, Jeff. "Where AI Thrives, Religion May Struggle." The University of Chicago Booth School of Business, March 26, 2024. https://www.chicagobooth.edu/review/where-ai-thrives-religion-may-struggle.

works with reasonable, scientific ones.[1824] The impact of automation on religious faith may be related to what the researchers refer to as religion's "instrumental" value.[1825]

According to Jesuits ECE (2024), as technology becomes more integrated with mankind, religion must likewise deal with AI.[1826] It will surely contribute to a better understanding of global systems, including ecological, social, economic, and political.[1827] By combining this massive amount of data, an AI-powered "Gaia twin," an omniscient system that predicts not just weather and climate but also human behavior, might be constructed.[1828] This system appears to be close to divine omniscience, as it knows everything—including the future.[1829] Such a technology, which outperforms the powers commonly attributed to God, has the potential to challenge traditional religious beliefs.[1830] Individuals in Islam and Christianity, for example, retain the freedom to select their religion, yet an AI algorithm may anticipate how people act and potentially impact choices.[1831]

According to the Church of Jesus Christ of Latter-Day Saints (2024), the Mormons will use AI to supplement, not replace, the relationship between God and his children.[1832] AI shall be used in constructive, helpful, and uplifting ways that uphold Latter-Day Saints (LDS) values and standards, including honesty, integrity, and ethics.[1833] People that interact with the organization would recognize that they are communicating with AI.[1834] It would disclose acknowledgment for AI-generated content if its legitimacy, accuracy, or authorship could be misinterpreted or misleading.[1835] The church's employment of AI would protect both sacred and personal information.[1836] It shall employ AI in accordance with the LDS policies and all applicable laws.[1837]

[1824] Ibid.

[1825] Ibid.

[1826] Jesuits ECE. "Religion Should Engage with Technology and AI." SJ Europe, September 2, 2024. https://jesuits.eu/news/2783-religion-should-engage-with-technology-and-ai.

[1827] Ibid.

[1828] Ibid.

[1829] Ibid.

[1830] Ibid.

[1831] Ibid.

[1832] The Church of Jesus Christ of Latter-Day Saints. "Guiding Principles for the Church's Use of Artificial Intelligence." newsroom.churchofjesuschrist.org, March 13, 2024. https://newsroom.churchofjesuschrist.org/article/church-jesus-christ-artificial-intelligence.

[1833] Ibid.

[1834] Ibid.

[1835] Ibid.

[1836] Ibid.

[1837] Ibid.

LDS sees various prospects for AI, notably in ancestral genealogy, expediting and streamlining operations, and a large possibility for translation to and interpretation within a different language.[1838] Generative AI might additionally provide Mormons natural language inquiries and prompts to seek up-to-date, precise data from recognized, solid, and authorized religious resources.[1839]

According to Cannon (2024), Mormons have traditionally been early users of technology, enthusiastically contributing to innovation in an effort to participate in God's work.[1840] Of course, such effort should reflect knowledge and inspiration, demonstrating honesty, cooperation with ethical government, and compassion for all.[1841] Mormons usually accept the notion of eternal progression.[1842] The ideology asserts that growth and learning are important components of human nature, now and forever, even if and when they reach superhuman or heavenly levels.[1843] So, it is hardly unexpected that LDS has taken a positive posture toward AI, viewing it as an ally rather than a foe.[1844] If AI can assist them in growing and learning, it should be considered one of the paths of eternal growth, if not ultimate exaltation into Godhood.[1845]

The church's teachings are consistent with Mormon Transhumanism, which envisions a future in which humans overcome biological restrictions through technology, combining scientific reasoning with spiritual enlightenment.[1846] Mormon transhumanists see technological breakthroughs that promise to transform human capacity, including but not limited to AI, as fulfillment of prophesy.[1847] They give Mormons active hope for a better future beyond current concepts of hatred, poverty, and death.[1848]

Jewish philosophy takes a distinct approach, according to Kalman (2024).[1849] Physical humans have limitless worth, yet that worth is linked with what Judaism considers to be human, with varying

---

[1838] Ibid.

[1839] Ibid.

[1840] Cannon, Lincoln. "The Church on Artificial Intelligence." Lincoln Cannon, July 7, 2024. https://lincoln.metacannon.net/2024/03/church-on-artificial-intelligence.html.

[1841] Ibid.

[1842] Ibid.

[1843] Ibid.

[1844] Ibid.

[1845] Ibid.

[1846] Ibid.

[1847] Ibid.

[1848] Ibid.

[1849] Kalman, David Zvi. "On AI, Jewish Thought Has Something Distinct to Say." Future of Life Institute, September 6, 2024. https://futureoflife.org/religion/ai-in-jewish-thought/.

degrees of personhood achievable in liminal instances.[1850] This perspective is responsible for the religion's nuanced approach to abortion, amongst other factors.[1851] This implies that they must carefully investigate granting a certain form of personality to robots that pose as humans.[1852] One clear downside of this strategy is that it can be utilized to dehumanize disabled individuals.[1853] As a result, the Jewish perspective should be stressed as a mixed, which having physical humanity and humane behavioral tendencies both influencing how they regard beings and technologies.[1854]

Within the Jewish faith, textual reading is more than merely an instrument for grasping the history; it is an observance in and of itself, a practice that all Jews (even though substantially more males than females) are urged to undertake throughout the course of their lives.[1855] The urge to learn difficult writings in Aramaic, pre-modern Hebrew, and various other languages has resulted in a particularly fruitful link between the Torah and technology.[1856] A few of Israel's earliest processors had been used to scan the sacred text to render it readily accessible, and the various electronic instruments accessible to users now is astounding.[1857] Nowadays, a great number of sacred writings are accessible for free on the internet, along with several versions and simple connections to browse this complex interconnected material.[1858] AI would most certainly be used in Jewish education soon.[1859] Generative AI now generates improved interpretations of the most challenging writings, and it may be utilized to assist trainees in navigating a big and chaotic library containing limited clear points of entry.[1860] In future generations, AI might enable students to interact with actual rabbis and literature from millennia before.[1861]

By exactly the same time, the ceremonial nature of Jewish education implies that AI reaches the *beit midrash* (study hall) sans fully dominating it.[1862] The capacity to comprehend the Talmud and Bible in the original languages they were written in, as well as *hevruta*—the practice of poring through books alongside a companion instead of isolation while in front of a monitor—are likely to remain

---

[1850] Ibid.
[1851] Ibid.
[1852] Ibid.
[1853] Ibid.
[1854] Ibid.
[1855] Ibid.
[1856] Ibid.
[1857] Ibid.
[1858] Ibid.
[1859] Ibid.
[1860] Ibid.
[1861] Ibid.
[1862] Ibid.

important aspects of text study.[1863] Jewish education additionally highlights interaction amongst academics and translators, whereas AI algorithms frequently fail to clarify how they understand what they perceive.[1864] Furthermore, Torah education stresses that holy writings are frequently multifaceted, multidimensional, and mysterious.[1865] The manner of perceiving literature is difficult to extract from AI algorithms, which are typically geared towards delivering brief and presumably full translations of original content.[1866] In fact, it implies the AI is going to join a long series of innovations which have enhanced Jewish education whilst preserving its forerunners.[1867] The contemporary *beit midrash* includes handmade scrolls of paper, hardcover publications, and monitors for computers.[1868] Everything maintains a space, and students can move amongst them whenever necessary.[1869]

According to Lad (2025), the connection between AI and Hindu scriptures provides an intriguing glimpse into the relationship between old wisdom and current technology.[1870] The Vedas and Upanishads are Hindu scriptures that explore the nature of awareness (Chaitanya) and intelligence.[1871] AI, albeit fake, can be considered as an expression of physical efforts to imitate and comprehend judgment.[1872] In Hinduism, the cosmos are frequently characterized to as the product by the holy intelligence (Brahman).[1873] In a similar vein, AI may be viewed as people imitating this artistic method through computers.[1874]

Karma (action and consequence) is an important concept in Hinduism.[1875] When designing and using AI, both individuals and worship facilities face moral obligation over the influence, in accordance to the karmic rule of guaranteeing that behaviors benefit others.[1876] AI may help to sustain dharma by tackling society issues like poverty, education, and healthcare.[1877]

[1863] Ibid.

[1864] Ibid.

[1865] Ibid.

[1866] Ibid.

[1867] Ibid.

[1868] Ibid.

[1869] Ibid.

[1870] Lad, Sagar. "The Spiritual Side of AI: AI and Consciousness." Medium, January 1, 2025. https://sagu94271.medium.com/the-spiritual-side-of-ai-ai-and-consciousness-237b1d374d1b.

[1871] Ibid.

[1872] Ibid.

[1873] Ibid.

[1874] Ibid.

[1875] Ibid.

[1876] Ibid.

[1877] Ibid.

The Hindu literature contains allusions to fake entities, that may be interpreted as the initial versions of AI.[1878] This false aspect of actuality, governed through supernatural beings, is similar to the way AI generates VR or AR.[1879] Older literature reference electronic gadgets called "yantras" which conducted duties, similar to machines or AI-powered devices presently.[1880] Both Devas (gods) and Asuras (demons) use advanced tools and knowledge, demonstrating how technology (including AI) can be used constructively or destructively.[1881]

Sanskrit, the original language used by several Hindu scriptures, is extremely organized and computer-friendly.[1882] Scientists looked into its usage in AI development, notably natural language processing (NLP).[1883] Panini's language (Ashtadhyayi), a centuries-old Sanskrit work, is regarded as to be among the first examples of computational thinking.[1884] The Hindu texts, which contain a precise concept categorization (for example, gunas, yugas, or ashramas), provide impetus for developing organized graphs of knowledge in AI platforms.[1885]

AI-powered wellness apps are incorporating Hindu scripture-based meditation and mindfulness practices.[1886] AI simulates practices borrowed from writings such as the Bhagavad Gita and Patanjali's Yoga Sutras to boost psychological health.[1887] Hindu philosophy examines several degrees of awareness, ranging from Jagrat (awake state) to Turiya (pure awakening).[1888] This may encourage AI investigations into replicating awareness states and comprehending how humans think.[1889]

Hindu scriptures frequently mention moksha (freedom) as the ultimate goal of existence.[1890] Avatar concepts (divine incarnations) may be used figuratively to describe AI-powered virtual beings which perform particular functions.[1891]

[1878] Ibid.
[1879] Ibid.
[1880] Ibid.
[1881] Ibid.
[1882] Ibid.
[1883] Ibid.
[1884] Ibid.
[1885] Ibid.
[1886] Ibid.
[1887] Ibid.
[1888] Ibid.
[1889] Ibid.
[1890] Ibid.
[1891] Ibid.

According to Walters (2023), artists and instructors are not the only ones concerned about breakthroughs in automation and AI.[1892] Robots are being introduced into Hinduism's most sacred rites, and not all believers are happy about it.[1893] In 2017, an Indian technology startup produced an autonomous arm to execute out "aarti," a rite whereby a worshiper presents a burning oil lamp to the god to represent the elimination of gloom.[1894] The machine was presented at the Ganpati festival, an annual event of multitudes of individuals where an idol of Ganesha, the elephant-headed deity, is carried forth in a parade and submerged in the Mula-Mutha river in Pune, Central India.[1895]

After that time, the mechanical aarti arm has spawned multiple models, some of them are still performing the ritual on a daily basis in India today, as well as various other religious robots in East and South Asia.[1896] In Kerala, India's southern coast, an animatronic temple elephant is still employed in robotic rites.[1897]

However, this type of religious robotics application has sparked heated arguments on the usage of AI and robotics in commitment and devotion.[1898] Some adherents and clergy believe that this development marks an era of change of individual ingenuity that could benefit the community, whereas other individuals are concerned that deploying machines instead of human gurus is an adverse sign for the years to come.[1899]

Ritual automation is the concept of AI religious activity and is not novel in South Asian faiths.[1900] Traditionally, it has encompassed everything between particular basins which pour water continuously for Hindu deity symbol washing rituals known as abhisheka to wind-powered Buddhist prayer wheels, which may be seen in supply stores and yoga studios.[1901] Although the modern form of computerized rituals may resemble installing an application for smartphones that sings mantras sans the use of a religious item, such as a mala or rosary, such novel ritual-performing robots have sparked heated debates.[1902]

[1892] Walters, Holly. "Robots Are Performing Hindu Rituals. Some Worshippers Fear They'll Be Replaced." PBS, March 11, 2023. https://www.pbs.org/newshour/world/robots-are-performing-hindu-rituals-some-worshippers-fear-theyll-be-replaced.

[1893] Ibid.
[1894] Ibid.
[1895] Ibid.
[1896] Ibid.
[1897] Ibid.
[1898] Ibid.
[1899] Ibid.
[1900] Ibid.
[1901] Ibid.
[1902] Ibid.

However, the growing application of AI and machinery within ceremonies of faith has raised anxieties amongst Hindus and Buddhists regarding the type of foreseeable future that robotics may bring.[1903] On certain cases, Hindus dispute if computerized spirituality heralds the entry of humankind onto a vibrant, fresh technology era or whether this is merely proof for an impending doomsday.[1904] For some circumstances, there are additionally worries about the expansion of machinery would result in a higher number of individuals abandoning faith, as temples depend on technology instead of clergy who care for their idols.[1905] Many of those worries originate on the realization that numerous faiths, across Southern Asia and around the world, have suffered a considerable decline over the amount of adolescents eager to devote themselves to religious instruction or devotion over recent decades.[1906] In addition, having numerous households residing in exile all over the globe, clergy or "pandits" are frequently leading increasingly smaller congregations.[1907] However, many people are unconvinced that ritual automation would benefit them.[1908] Furthermore, they challenge the simultaneous use of artificial gods to represent and reflect the transcendent, because these depictions are created by humans and hence represent the beliefs held by the designers.[1909]

Zheng (2024) defines Humanistic Buddhism as an amalgam of the mainstreams of contemporary Buddhism, focusing on its humanistic aspect.[1910] As AI technology advances, Humanistic Buddhism is also modernizing and evolving, resulting in a perpetual confrontation between religious beliefs and technological breakthroughs.[1911]

One of the most common institutions of modern Buddhism is humanistic Buddhism.[1912] The origins of it and growth have linked to the evolution of modernism.[1913] The goal is to modernize Buddhism at both the doctrinal and institutional levels, adapting it to contemporary society and

---

[1903] Ibid.

[1904] Ibid.

[1905] Ibid.

[1906] Ibid.

[1907] Ibid.

[1908] Ibid.

[1909] Ibid.

[1910] Zheng, Yutong. "Buddhist Transformation in the Digital Age: AI (Artificial Intelligence) and Humanistic Buddhism." *Religions* 15, no. 1 (January 9, 2024): 79. https://doi.org/10.3390/rel15010079.

[1911] Ibid.

[1912] Ibid.

[1913] Ibid.

conceptions, and ensuring its survival and progress.[1914] The term "Humanistic Buddhism" originated in the early 1900s.[1915] During that period, Chinese society was experiencing significant transformations, government control was dwindling, and there was widespread unrest.[1916] The emergence of "democracy" and "science" led to a social movement against religion and superstition.[1917] However, intellectuals questioned the importance of faith.[1918] Chinese Buddhism had been in decay and nearly lost its cultural responsibilities.[1919] Buddhist thinkers recognized the need to revitalize and adapt Buddhism to modern culture, aiming to develop it in new ways.[1920]

Humanistic Buddhism aims to modernize Buddhism and promote societal development.[1921] It has also paved the way for the technologicalization of Humanistic Buddhism.[1922] Using AI tools at different levels reflects a global mindset and adaptability to current needs.[1923] AI was recently utilized to advance Humanistic Buddhism, including AI monks, scriptural interpretation, and online Buddhist communities via the web.[1924]

[1914] Ibid.
[1915] Ibid.
[1916] Ibid.
[1917] Ibid.
[1918] Ibid.
[1919] Ibid.
[1920] Ibid.
[1921] Ibid.
[1922] Ibid.
[1923] Ibid.
[1924] Ibid.

10 AUTOPILOT

I have a fear of flying. After learning that AI is involved in airline operations, I would be less comfortable boarding one in the future.

According to Sahota (2024), the airline business, which is recognized for its intricate structure and elevated logistical requests, has begun to depend on AI to improve productivity, security, and consumer happiness.[1925] AI's capability to interpret massive volumes of information quickly and precisely has proven essential in tackling the particular issues of flying.[1926]

AI plays an important role in enhancing aircraft procedures and security.[1927] As an instance, Boeing employs AI within its Airplane Health Management framework, that observes airplanes during transit and forecasts possible problems with maintenance prior to becoming a problem.[1928] The proactive strategy maximizes operating effectiveness as well as security.[1929] A different instance is Airbus's Skywise, an online system which employs AI to evaluate onboard information.[1930] The method aids to maximize aircraft paths, lowers emissions, and increases the whole operating efficiency.[1931] Skywise can identify potential delays or technical concerns, allowing for proactive mitigation.[1932]

[1925] Sahota, Neil. "Navigating the Skies with AI: How Airlines Are Transforming Air Travel." Forbes, March 29, 2024. https://www.forbes.com/sites/neilsahota/2024/03/29/navigating-the-skies-with-ai-how-airlines-are-transforming-air-travel/.

[1926] Ibid.
[1927] Ibid.
[1928] Ibid.
[1929] Ibid.
[1930] Ibid.
[1931] Ibid.
[1932] Ibid.

Unexpectedly, perhaps, airliners employ AI to improve client satisfaction and participation.[1933] AI chatbots are becoming more frequent on airline portals and smartphone applications.[1934] Companies help consumers through requests, reservations, and modifications to flights round the clock, delivering an efficient and straightforward to use service.[1935] KLM's chatbot, BlueBot, is a perfect example because it aids travelers with booking and information about flights through Facebook Messenger.[1936] AI is additionally utilized to tailor the consumer interactions.[1937] Delta Air Lines, for instance, employs AI to provide tailored onboard amenities according to passengers' interests.[1938]

AI is improving luggage control and operations at airports.[1939] SITA, an airline IT business, created an AI-driven luggage management tool to reduce baggage loss incidences.[1940] The technology gives immediate updates about luggage position, considerably improving the traveler's journey while lowering operating expenses.[1941] AI is utilized in airport operations to manage crowds and ensure security.[1942] Some airports, such as Delta's biometric terminals in Atlanta and Minneapolis, already use facial recognition technology for rapid and secure boarding.[1943]

AI-powered predictive maintenance transforms aviation maintenance and repair.[1944] Programs use information collected by airplane monitors to forecast whenever components require to be serviced or replaced.[1945] The proactive method, so compared to maintenance that is reactive, reduces delay and increases airplane dependability.[1946] EasyJet, for instance, utilizes AI to anticipate part substitutions, which reduces cancellations and postponements caused by mechanical issues.[1947]

According to Miller, Holley, and Halawi (2023), AI is rapidly evolving as a technology with the

---

[1933] Ibid.
[1934] Ibid.
[1935] Ibid.
[1936] Ibid.
[1937] Ibid.
[1938] Ibid.
[1939] Ibid.
[1940] Ibid.
[1941] Ibid.
[1942] Ibid.
[1943] Ibid.
[1944] Ibid.
[1945] Ibid.
[1946] Ibid.
[1947] Ibid.

potential to transform into numerous key applications in various industries, including commercial aviation.[1948] Global AI spending is expected to reach $204 billion in 2025, up from $80 billion in 2021.[1949] AI in aviation is expected to increase from $653.74 million in 2021 to $9,985.85 million by 2030, with a compound annual growth rate of 35.38% from 2022 to 2030.[1950] Research and development in the aviation industry is backed by increased investments and a growing need for AI applications, aligning with expectations.[1951]

It is unclear how the specific usage will be incorporated.[1952] Wherever AI may dwell aboard a highly sophisticated control platform whereas pilots constantly manage effective aircraft procedures under security limitations, along with the way pilots may react to novel AI deployment, pose critical problems.[1953] A relevant topic is whether pilots in the US aviation sector are prepared and motivated to embrace emerging AI technology as front-line controllers.[1954] In a similar vein it is possible to wonder if adoption will require significant duration and shifts in culture for pilots trusting AI as credible upgrades to the digital flight deck (DFD).[1955]

While AI offers immense promise of improving a pilot's job in air travel, but presents numerous fresh moral, community, and technical obstacles.[1956] Trustworthy AI (TAI) believes that confidence represents the basis that supports neighborhoods, the economy, and sustainable development.[1957] Regarding commercial airlines, DFD faith in AI is both an opinion and an obstacle in crucial airline security domains.[1958] In the United States, TAI has served as the basis for security advancements during the previous 50 years, transforming commercial airplanes into the safest source of transport.[1959] The TIA limitation has several critical elements:

[1948] Miller, Mark, Sam Holley, and Leila Halawi. "The Evolution of AI on the Commercial Flight Deck: Finding Balance between Efficiency and Safety While Maintaining the Integrity of Operator Trust." *AHFE International* 13 (2023): 14. https://doi.org/10.54941/ahfe1004175.

[1949] Ibid.
[1950] Ibid.
[1951] Ibid.
[1952] Ibid.
[1953] Ibid.
[1954] Ibid.
[1955] Ibid.
[1956] Ibid.
[1957] Ibid.
[1958] Ibid.
[1959] Ibid.

- The Federal Aviation Administration (FAA) provides significant regulation and monitoring.[1960]

- The National Transportation Safety Board provides precise and trustworthy crash investigation information as well as suggestions.[1961]

- The Air Transport Association (ATA) represents a huge commercial aviation company conglomerate.[1962]

- The Air Line Pilots Association (ALPA) has a significant depiction of commercial airline pilots in the United States.[1963]

- Manufacturers' cooperation is essential.[1964]

Companies and society in the commercial aircraft industry will reach all that is possible of AI when sufficient confidence in its research, delivery, and trustworthy application is established.[1965] As commercial flying becomes more focused on vital operations to maintain aircraft flying safely and efficiently, pilots face more risk in effectively resolving any abnormalities or system interruptions.[1966] To achieve FAA certification, AI should properly integrate into other robotic and electronic devices utilized in commercial DFDs.[1967] Any alteration or deviation from TAI could result in major ramifications for an industry that depends on both security and effectiveness to generate income.[1968] To appreciate why TIA is essential for commercial aviation and pilots, it is important to recognize that the primary threat is human error, not technological failure.[1969] Human error accounts for 80% of all commercial aviation accidents in the United States.[1970] Implementing new AI on the DFD requires HF expertise to prevent mistakes by humans.[1971]

Commercial passenger travel increased considerably in the post-World War II era as jet engines became more reliable, reached higher speeds, and flew more smoothly.[1972] After the Boeing 707's maiden commercial flight in 1958, there was a dramatic decrease in commercial aviation accidents

---

[1960] Ibid.
[1961] Ibid.
[1962] Ibid.
[1963] Ibid.
[1964] Ibid.
[1965] Ibid.
[1966] Ibid.
[1967] Ibid.
[1968] Ibid.
[1969] Ibid.
[1970] Ibid.
[1971] Ibid.
[1972] Ibid.

due to aircraft problems throughout the next decade.[1973] However, mishaps remained due to human mistake on the flight deck.[1974] Controlled Flight into Terrain (CFIT) is a prevalent global aviation safety issue caused by these errors.[1975] The bulk of commercial CFIT incidents are caused by human mistake, prompting the industry to seek technology solutions on the flight deck.[1976] This was a restricted kind of AI known as the Ground Proximity Warning System (GPWS), which the FAA currently classifies as a Terrain Awareness Warning System (TAWS).[1977] By 1974, the FAA mandated that all big U.S. aircraft install GPWS.[1978] According to a 2006 assessment, there is not one traveler death in a major American commercial airliner as an outcome of a CFIT incident in the US since 1974.[1979] During the point of the GPWS adoption, commercial aviation flight cabin automation was restricted to Autopilot, the Flight Management System (FMS), and automated Flight Control Systems (FCS).[1980] The GPWS had a radio barometer that indicated the plane's height over ground level, pattern computation, and warnings for the airline crew via audio and visual signals (a total of seven) when the plane was operating in extremely dangerous situations.[1981] Voice-generated alerts was issued for rapid lineage, topographical closing, and clearing velocity.[1982] Notices got issued for risky topographical passage and severe departure beyond glideslope.[1983] This was an innovative type of specific AI that increased pilots' situational awareness (SA) of the topographical area.[1984] However, pilots did not immediately trust it completely.[1985]

Unreliability caused by a blind area was one of the flaws that contributed to GPWS's lack of confidence in the 1970s and 1980s.[1986] The system could only collect information immediately underneath the plane, leading to a deficiency in forecasting ahead topographical characteristics as well as a failure to estimate closing stages, which would allow for avoidance actions.[1987] Ultimately, multi-crew personnel acquired proper instruction and was bound by law to act whenever a GPWS alarm was generated.[1988] Yet, under heavy-workload scenarios, GPWS notifications may

---

[1973] Ibid.
[1974] Ibid.
[1975] Ibid.
[1976] Ibid.
[1977] Ibid.
[1978] Ibid.
[1979] Ibid.
[1980] Ibid.
[1981] Ibid.
[1982] Ibid.
[1983] Ibid.
[1984] Ibid.
[1985] Ibid.
[1986] Ibid.
[1987] Ibid.
[1988] Ibid.

surprise and confuse the crew's responses.[1989] To eliminate the blind spot, Enhanced GPWS (EGPWS) and Terrain Awareness Warning System (TAWS) were put in on commercial aircraft in the United States in the 1990s.[1990] The EGPWS trend processor compares the aircraft's GPS position to the terrain dataset.[1991] This is supported with a landscape screen which assists pilots understand their surroundings and reduces the risk of falling low.[1992] The enhancements increased alert durations and reduced delayed reactions by pilots.[1993] EGPWS equipment has advanced and is now basic TAI gear for the DFD.[1994] The dependability of EGPWS led to TAI and decreased CFITs globally.[1995] Further development needed to be made in the human-machine interface (HMI) to improve user confidence and reliability.[1996]

Kumar (2022) reports that the COVID-19 pandemic was having a significant impact on the airline industry, leading to reduced traffic for passengers, air freight demand, airport workers, and incoming income.[1997] However, the situation is stabilizing, although more challenges remain.[1998] Aviation accounts for about a third of worldwide trade, making it a crucial sector of the global economy and business.[1999] The aviation sector employs 13.5 million individuals globally and generates approximately $880 billion to global GDP annually.[2000]

Modern technical advancements are significantly impacting the airline and aviation industries.[2001] Emerging technology is enabling exponential growth in various industries, including aviation.[2002] New technologies, including AI, robots, IoT, aircraft systems, and hybrid/electric aircraft, are transforming the aerospace business.[2003]

AI can benefit commercial air travel in additional ways. Abubakar, et al. (2022) found that as the

---

[1989] Ibid.

[1990] Ibid.

[1991] Ibid.

[1992] Ibid.

[1993] Ibid.

[1994] Ibid.

[1995] Ibid.

[1996] Ibid.

[1997] Kumar, Mahesh. "Optimized Application of Artificial Intelligence (AI) in Aviation Market." *International Journal of Recent Research Aspects* 9, no. 4 (December 2022): p. 1.

[1998] Ibid.

[1999] Ibid.

[2000] Ibid.

[2001] Ibid.

[2002] Ibid.

[2003] Ibid.

aviation sector grows, there is a preference for cost-effective and durable plane components.[2004] Useful applications were created to help find new ways to design aviation parts.[2005] AI, particularly ML, enables the development of hitherto impossible applications.[2006] Automakers can create components using a combination of generative structures and AI algorithms.[2007] AI gives engineers and constructors with options for the most convenient time to accomplish the best design.[2008] AI-driven adaptive modeling and three-dimensional manufacturing may produce components such as wings and propellers.[2009] AI optimization could improve the production and process of design in the airline industry.[2010] Engineers are responsible for designing airplanes, including determining their size.[2011] Traditional mathematical modeling has relied on theoretical methodologies for a long time.[2012] However, because theory is not grounded in reality, errors are inevitable.[2013] ML can help bring conceptions closer to reality.[2014] The Boeing 777 was the first digitally designed airplane using 3D solids technology, serving as a classic example.[2015] The airplane was designed on a computer, eliminating the necessity for costly full-scale mock-ups.[2016]

Historically, the airline sector has profited from declines on oil and jet fuel prices.[2017] Kerosene currently accounts for 19.5% of total aircraft operation expenses, up from 16% in 2016.[2018] As the cost of kerosene increases, also does the demand for a precise evaluation of airplane gas consumption.[2019] Reduced gasoline usage benefits both the business and the environment.[2020] A Boeing 747 airliner uses four gallons every second.[2021] As a result, the airplane would require 150,000 gallons of gasoline throughout a 10-hour voyage.[2022]

[2004] Abubakar, Mahmoud, Odunlami EriOluwa, Mangai Teyei, and Fadi Al-Turjman. "AI application in the aviation sector." In *2022 International Conference on Artificial Intelligence of Things and Crowdsensing (AIoTCs)*, pp. 53. IEEE, 2022.
[2005] Ibid.
[2006] Ibid.
[2007] Ibid.
[2008] Ibid.
[2009] Ibid.
[2010] Ibid.
[2011] Ibid.
[2012] Ibid.
[2013] Ibid.
[2014] Ibid.
[2015] Ibid.
[2016] Ibid.
[2017] Ibid.
[2018] Ibid.
[2019] Ibid.
[2020] Ibid.
[2021] Ibid.
[2022] Ibid.

AI-driven equipment can reduce fuel consumption by airplanes.[2023] AI assists pilots in analyzing critical flight data, including gasoline framework, equipment condition, the climate, and various other elements, to improve performance.[2024] Safety Line, a French company, created a ML technology to assist pilots in their career progression.[2025] Air Alaska conserved about 1,820,000 gallons of gasoline in the span of six months by using the Flyways program for arranging flights.[2026] Furthermore, 4,600 tons of greenhouse gases was avoided.[2027]

Airports are often overcrowded due to the high volume of international travelers.[2028] Controlling air traffic is crucial to avoid catastrophic accidents caused by jet crashes.[2029] AI can help handle complex air traffic, making it a viable solution.[2030] AI and ML algorithms can help pilots and detect traffic.[2031] Modern airplanes receive fairly extensive and comprehensive information from various plane locations and subsystems thanks to a range of sensors.[2032] This data can be used for in-flight tracking and post-trip performance assessments.[2033] AI assistants can help pilots make intelligent judgments according to the weather and flight data.[2034] In case of extreme storms, the AI assistants may direct pilots to take different itineraries.[2035] AI can recognize when two airplanes are on an identical direction, enabling air traffic controllers to notify pilots by instructing them to drop elevation.[2036] Air traffic controllers may also monitor flights as they leave or approach the runway using AI and smart cameras.[2037]

AI can use computer vision, spatial signal processing, and advanced analytics to detect and categorize risks and hazards.[2038] Satellites and drones give image and video data for AI systems to learn from.[2039] The AI can evaluate surveillance footage to determine if it is normal or potentially

---

[2023] Ibid.
[2024] Ibid.
[2025] Ibid., p. 53-54
[2026] Ibid., p. 54
[2027] Ibid.
[2028] Ibid.
[2029] Ibid.
[2030] Ibid.
[2031] Ibid.
[2032] Ibid.
[2033] Ibid.
[2034] Ibid.
[2035] Ibid.
[2036] Ibid.
[2037] Ibid.
[2038] Ibid.
[2039] Ibid.

dangerous.[2040] AI enables the Aircraft Real-Time Health Monitoring System (ARHMS).[2041] Instruments mounted throughout the airplane monitor and process differences in temperature, pressure, electromagnetic power, and moisture.[2042] After landing, the airplane is scanned and tested using ARHMS to avoid unexpected disasters.[2043]

One of the most pressing problems in airplane travel is safety.[2044] AI is used at airports to guarantee passenger security by detecting suspicious individuals utilizing facial monitoring.[2045] Data from individuals with criminal records can train AI systems to detect criminal activities.[2046] Passenger identification is becoming easier as airport officials spend less time authenticating a person's identity.[2047] Safety has improved primarily an outcome of the deployment of biometric scanning and technologies for facial recognition, that have almost removed terrorists' capacity to travel and cause chaos.[2048]

Long check-in lineups at airports are a major source of pain during plane travel.[2049] Passengers often spend long periods of time waiting in line for service.[2050] Commercial aviation relies heavily on client satisfaction and service excellence.[2051] AI can help airlines improve consumer engagement and service quality.[2052] Airlines provide self-check-in services via their websites.[2053] To enhance the passenger experience at airports, personal assistant robots are stationed at certain locations.[2054] In some airports, customers can use self-service devices to obtain boarding tickets.[2055] All of this is made possible via AI.[2056]

AI is also employed in flight instruction.[2057] Flying students become immersed in AI simulators

---

[2040] Ibid.
[2041] Ibid.
[2042] Ibid.
[2043] Ibid.
[2044] Ibid.
[2045] Ibid.
[2046] Ibid.
[2047] Ibid.
[2048] Ibid.
[2049] Ibid.
[2050] Ibid.
[2051] Ibid.
[2052] Ibid.
[2053] Ibid.
[2054] Ibid.
[2055] Ibid.
[2056] Ibid.
[2057] Ibid.

that combine with engaging digital environments to replicate a realistic experience.[2058] Biometrics along with other academic data can additionally be collected and analyzed using simulators with AI abilities to create tailored learning programs according to the student's level of achievement.[2059] AI is used in the cockpit to assist pilots during their flight.[2060] AI within the cockpit helps pilots optimize their flying paths by reviewing and notifying users regarding atmospheric conditions, gas levels, and additional considerations.[2061] Boeing's MCAS increased the plane's pitch stabilization.[2062] MCAS corrects any inaccuracies in Angle of Attack (AOA) sensor information in this scenario.[2063] Following thorough study and evaluation, the system will undergo verification exercises with FAA experts throughout during flight examination prior to being completion.[2064]

[2058] Ibid.

[2059] Ibid.

[2060] Ibid.

[2061] Ibid.

[2062] Ibid.

[2063] Ibid.

[2064] Ibid.

11 AI IN PHOTOGRAPHY

According to Pestano (2024), AI has made advances in photography over the past few years, altering how individuals handle the craft of image capture.[2065] Perhaps the more prominent applications of AI in photography involves the automation of picture processing.[2066] Photographers can now use AI-powered algorithms that autonomously alter the lighting, contrast, and balance of colors to produce further appealing photographs.[2067] It allows novice photographers to create professionally-appealing photographs without dealing with complex post-processing processes.[2068] Furthermore, AI may assist professional photographers streamline their processes by outsourcing monotonous duties autonomously, permitting them to concentrate on more innovative areas of their occupation.[2069]

A different manner AI is changing photography is by using ML techniques.[2070] By studying large image collections, AI may learn to detect and differentiate between a variety of items.[2071] It may be employed to construct specially personalized picture detection systems which assist photographers in identifying particular settings or items and making better judgments regarding how to photograph these.[2072]

AI is also utilized to improve the quality and accuracy of pictures.[2073] DL techniques enable AI products to automatically detect and eliminate undesirable noise and artifacts that can degrade

---

[2065] Pestano, Dane. "AI in Photography - the Good, the Bad and the Ugly." Professional Photo, January 24, 2024. https://professionalphoto.online/ai-artificial-intelligence/ai-in-photography-the-good-the-bad-and-the-ugly/.

[2066] Ibid.
[2067] Ibid.
[2068] Ibid.
[2069] Ibid.
[2070] Ibid.
[2071] Ibid.
[2072] Ibid.
[2073] Ibid.

image quality.[2074] Additionally, AI can be utilized to improve image detail and sharpness, resulting in crisper and more colorful photographs.[2075] As a result, AI is increasingly becoming a crucial tool for photographers of all skill levels.[2076] As AI advances, photographers may anticipate even more interesting discoveries in this discipline, ushering in an age of photography which becomes more innovative, productive, and influential than at any point previously.[2077]

Photographs created with AI are gaining popularity because of their capacity to improve photos and provide high-quality outcomes.[2078] In contrast, raw photos have not been edited and capture the image exactly as it appears at the time of capture.[2079] Although all styles of photography have merits, however, there is a rising discussion about how images created through AI ought to be distinguished from natural or human-assisted pictures.[2080] Many suggest that AI-assisted photos ought to be properly identified accordingly, whereas other people consider that the difference is irrelevant.[2081]

The primary argument in the direction of distinguishing AI-assisted images is the fact that they can create a misleading sense of realism.[2082] AI algorithms may edit photographs by changing their colors, adding or removing objects, or even creating totally new ones.[2083] Although it might be beneficial for creative objectives, it may also be deceptive when a person believes that they are viewing an unedited shot.[2084] Others say that the whole point of photographing is to record an event or convey an account, and AI can help with such.[2085]

AI-assisted images can provide a more accurate portrayal of the captured moment by boosting colors, changing focus, or improving sharpness.[2086] Finally, whether AI-assisted photographs ought to be distinguished from the original images remains up for discussion.[2087] Although there may be good reasons from the two sides, the primary objective is for photographers to remain open

---

[2074] Ibid.
[2075] Ibid.
[2076] Ibid.
[2077] Ibid.
[2078] Ibid.
[2079] Ibid.
[2080] Ibid.
[2081] Ibid.
[2082] Ibid.
[2083] Ibid.
[2084] Ibid.
[2085] Ibid.
[2086] Ibid.
[2087] Ibid.

regarding their methods along with for spectators to have an understanding of the possible drawbacks of AI-assisted imagery.[2088]

Nevertheless, an ongoing issue is that AI is current emerging in various photography programs.[2089] One of them is Adobe Photoshop's AI-powered tools, including Adobe Sensei, which can be utilized to perform jobs such as object selection and masking, image enhancement, and alternative composition generation.[2090] Skylum Luminar enhances photos with AI-powered editing tools, such as the AI Sky Enhancer and AI Structure.[2091] Topaz Labs provides numerous AI-powered photo editing software plugins, including Topaz AI Gigapixel, which allows the photographer to enlarge photographs without compromising quality, and Topaz Sharpen AI, which corrects fuzzy photos.[2092] Google Photos employs AI to automatically enhance and organize photographs, such as changing lighting, color balance, and contrast.[2093] DxO PhotoLab has AI-powered tools like DxO Smart Lighting, which can automatically change contrast and exposure in photographs.[2094] These can be considered merely a few instances of photography applications that uses AI to enhance its enhancement and modification processes.[2095] As AI evolves and improves, more photography software is likely to include AI-powered tools and capabilities.[2096]

It is critical for photography contests to establish defined regulations and criteria regarding the usage of AI in photography.[2097] Competitions, for instance, may mandate photographers to be transparent on the use of AI in their entries, as well as that any photographs submitted were not extensively modified or made totally using AI algorithms.[2098]

Judges ought to also be trained in the usage of AI in photographs should have the ability to tell whether a picture is primarily genuine or entirely AI-generated.[2099] Furthermore, photography contests must take into consideration introducing different categories for AI-assisted photography, as it might not be suitable to compare the photos directly to raw shots.[2100] This might assist to

[2088] Ibid.
[2089] Ibid.
[2090] Ibid.
[2091] Ibid.
[2092] Ibid.
[2093] Ibid.
[2094] Ibid.
[2095] Ibid.
[2096] Ibid.
[2097] Ibid.
[2098] Ibid.
[2099] Ibid.
[2100] Ibid.

guarantee that all photographs are judged on an equal footing and that the usage of AI is not unfairly favored or penalized.[2101] AI photographs, overall, may be accepted in photo competitions if they are judged honestly and openly, and organizers and judges create explicit standards for utilization.[2102]

Clearly, there are reservations regarding AI's ability to completely substitute human photographers.[2103] Although AI may be utilized to streamline specific processes to boost productivity, many are concerned that it would devalue the human capacity for perception and imagination in photography, affecting the bottom line and photographers' livelihoods.[2104] Regardless of the method chosen, a distinct benefit for human photography over AI is the fact that humans are creative and may add a distinct aesthetic viewpoint to their work.[2105] Individuals might additionally utilize perception to detect instances that AI might miss.[2106] Furthermore, humans may modify their photographic techniques and equipment to suit various settings, such as poor lighting or objects that move quickly, something AI might have trouble with.[2107] Lastly, photographers can form personal connections between the people they photograph, resulting in more meaningful and emotionally charged photos.[2108]

Before Trump took the oath of office for his second term in 2025, official portraits of him and Vice President J.D. Vance were released to the media. I became convinced that they look AI-generated, which would be very inappropriate for the highest office in the country. It reminded me of Trump's mugshot when he was prosecuted for the Georgia election interference in 2023. I am trying to dig into some information behind the portraits.

According to Lapham (2025), a former White House photographer, Trump's portrait was substantially modified after the shoot, using both studio lighting and retouching techniques.[2109] The photo appears to employ "monster" lighting to drastically highlight the president from below and make his eyes stand out.[2110] The lighting gives the image an "ominous" appearance, as seen in horror films.[2111] She compared Trump's portrayal to that of a boxer about to fight.[2112]

[2101] Ibid.
[2102] Ibid.
[2103] Ibid.
[2104] Ibid.
[2105] Ibid.
[2106] Ibid.
[2107] Ibid.
[2108] Ibid.
[2109] Ibid.
[2110] Ibid.
[2111] Ibid.
[2112] Ibid.

During the 2024 election season, various candidates have used AI to disseminate information about their opponent or to use fake objects to motivate their election message. According to Jingnan (2024), photographs depicting the destruction caused by Hurricane Helene circulated on the internet, as was a photograph of a grieving toddler carrying a dog on a boat.[2113] A few posts on X that featured the photo gained millions of hits.[2114] Many users reacted emotionally, especially a number of Republicans who wanted to condemn the Biden administration's response to catastrophes.[2115] However, others swiftly identified clear signals that the photograph was probably created using generative AI techniques, such as deformed limbs and blurriness, which are prevalent among AI image generators.[2116] During the election campaign, AI-powered fake pictures flourished on social networking platforms, typically following heated reports.[2117] Individuals who are carefully following the election on internet platforms believe that the photos were used to create biased accounts, with irrelevant facts.[2118] After users using X wrote a collective message indicating the photo of the youngster in the boat was AI-generated, the individuals who posted it, including Sen. Mike Lee (R-Utah), erased their postings.[2119] This is considered political propaganda.[2120]

In conclusion, AI is never intended to be genuine. As stated in my previous book, it will destroy the ways of life humans enjoyed, including jobs. The more jobs lost to AI, the more people who would go into poverty. Although the devices and features mentioned may help alleviate some stress, but it is not to be trusted for everyday use.

Bibliography

Abdollahi, Jafar, and Laya Mahmoudi. 2021. "Investigation of artificial intelligence in stock market prediction studies: Review." *10th International Conference on Innovation and Research in Engineering Sciences* 1-4. Accessed April 16, 2025.

[2113] Jingnan, Huo. "AI-Generated Images Have Become a New Form of Propaganda This Election Season." NPR, October 18, 2024. https://www.npr.org/2024/10/18/nx-s1-5153741/ai-images-hurricanes-disasters-propaganda.

[2114] Ibid.
[2115] Ibid.
[2116] Ibid.
[2117] Ibid.
[2118] Ibid.
[2119] Ibid.
[2120] Ibid.

Abubakar, Mahmoud, Odunlami EriOluwa, Mangai Teyer, and Fadi Al-Turjman. 2022. "AI Application in the Aviation Sector." *2022 International Conference on Artificial Intelligence of Things and Crowdsensing (AIoTCs)*. IEEE. 52-55. Accessed April 22, 2025. doi:10.1109/AIoTCs58181.2022.00015.

Adak, Anirban, Biswajeet Pradhan, and Nagesh Shukla. 2022. "Sentiment Analysis of Customer Reviews of Food Delivery Services Using Deep Learning and Explainable Artificial Intelligence: Systematic Review." *Foods* 11 (10): 1500. Accessed April 19, 2025. doi:10.3390/foods11101500.

Adanyin, Anthonette. 2024. "Ethical AI in Retail: Consumer Privacy and Fairness." *European Journal of Computer Science and Information Technology* 12 (7): 21-35. Accessed April 15, 2025. doi:10.37745/ejcsit.2013/vol12n72135.

Adebakin, Adeyinka. 2023. "Self-Checkout for what? An Exploration of the Usage and Adoption of Self-Checkouts Before and After the COVID-19 Pandemic." Research Paper, Technical University of Munich, 1-25. Accessed April 15, 2025. doi: 10.13140/RG.2.2.18559.38566.

Adeoye, Yetunde, Erumusele Francis Onotole, Tunde Ogunyankinnu, Godwin Apioh, Akintunde Akinyele Osunkanmibi, and Joseph Egbemhenghe. 2025. "Artificial Intelligence in Logistics and Distribution: The function of AI in dynamic route planning for transportation, including self-driving trucks and drone delivery systems." *World Journal of Advanced Research and Reviews* 25 (2): 155-167. Accessed April 12, 2025. doi:10.30574/wjarr.

Adler, Alan. 2023. *Feds close probe into TuSimple autonomous truck crash.* March 2. Accessed April 12, 2025. https://www.freightwaves.com/news/feds-close-probe-into-tusimple-autonomous-truck-crash.

Anica-Popa, Ionut, Liana Anica-Popa, Cristina Radulescu, and Marinela Vrincianu. 2021. "The integration of artificial intelligence in retail: Benefits, challenges and a dedicated conceptual framework." *Amfiteatru Economic Journal* 23 (56): 120-136. Accessed April 15, 2025. doi:10.24818/EA/2021/56/120.

Arasi, Munya A., Hussah Nasser AlEisa, Amani A. Alneil, and Radwa Marzouk. 2025. "Artificial intelligence-driven ensemble deep learning models for smart monitoring of indoor activities in IoT environment for people with disabilities." *Scientific Reports* 15 (1): 4337. Accessed April 12, 2025. doi:10.1038/s41598-025-88450-1.

Beck, Serge. 2024. *How Artificial Intelligence Is Reshaping Banking.* February 23. Accessed April 16, 2025. https://www.forbes.com/councils/forbestechcouncil/2024/02/23/how-artificial-intelligence-is-reshaping-banking/.

Bi, Shuochen, Wenqing Bao, Jue Xiao, Jiangshan Wang, and Tingting Deng. 2024. "Application and practice of AI technology in quantitative investment." *Information Systems and Economics* 5 (2): 124-132. Accessed April 16, 2025. doi:10.23977/infse.2024.050217.

Binkley, Charles E., Joel M. Reynolds, and Andrew G. Shuman. 2025. "Health AI poses distinct harms and potential benefits for people living with disabilities." *Nature Medicine* 1-2. Accessed April 12, 2025. doi:10.1038/s41591-024-03432-6.

Buehler, T. Leigh. 2024. *Artificial Intelligence in Retail and Improving Efficiency.* March 4. Accessed April 15, 2025. https://www.apu.apus.edu/area-of-study/business-and-management/resources/artificial-intelligence-in-retail-and-improving-efficiency/.

Burton, Bonnie. 2020. *This robot will give you a new haircut...if you dare.* July 22. Accessed April 16, 2025. https://www.cnet.com/science/this-robot-will-give-you-a-new-haircut-if-you-dare/.

Calo, Zachary R. 2024. "AI, medicine and Christian ethics." *Research Handbook on Health, AI and the Law* 219-233. Accessed April 22, 2025.

Cannon, Lincoln. 2024. *The Church on Artificial Intelligence.* July 7. Accessed April 22, 2025. https://lincoln.metacannon.net/2024/03/church-on-artificial-intelligence.html.

Caswell, David, and Mary Fitzgerald. 2025. *AI is the media's chance to reinvent itself.* March 5. Accessed April 18, 2025. https://www.prospectmagazine.co.uk/ideas/media/69423/artificial-intelligence-journalism-reinvention.

Chopra, Ritika, and Gagan Deep Sharma. 2021. "Application Artificial Intelligence in Stock Market Forecasting: A Critique, Review, and Research Agenda." *Journal of Risk and Financial Management* 14 (11): 526. Accessed April 17, 2025. doi:10.3390/jrfm14110526.

Chua, Alton Y.K., Anjan Pal, and Snehasish Banerjee. 2023. "AI-enabled investment advice: Will users buy it?" *Computers in Human Behavior* 138: 107481. Accessed April 16, 2025. doi:10.1016/j.chb.2022.107481.

Cockrell, Jeff. 2024. *Where AI Thrives, Religion May Struggle.* March 26. Accessed April 21, 2025. https://www.chicagobooth.edu/review/where-ai-thrives-religion-may-struggle.

Coghill, George M. 2023. "Artificial Intelligence (and Christianity): Who? What? Where? When? Why? and How?" *Studies in Christian Ethics* 36 (3): 604-619. Accessed April 20, 2025. doi:10.1177/09539468231169462.

Council, Stephen. 2023. *Bay Area-founded pizza startup Zume reportedly shuts down after raising $445 million.* June 5. Accessed April 25, 2025. https://www.sfgate.com/tech/article/zume-pizza-startup-shuts-down-18136126.php.

Davidson, Jess. 2025. *Report: Building A Disabiilty-InclusiveAI Ecosystem; A Cross-Disability, Cross-Systems Analysis of Best Practices.* March 11. Accessed April 12, 2025. https://www.aapd.com/disability-inclusive-ai/.

DeLuca, Renee. 2024. *Artificial Intelligence in the pulpit: a chruch service written entirely by AI.* July 16. Accessed April 20, 2025. https://www.ucc.org/artificial-intelligence-in-the-pulpit-a-church-service-written-entirely-by-ai/.

Dickinson, Grace. 2023. *How Do Robotic Waiters Work & Are They Right for Your Restaurant.* February 21. Accessed April 25, 2025. https://backofhouse.io/resources/how-do-robotic-waiters-work-and-are-they-right-for-your-restaurant.

Downie, Amanda, and Molly Hayes. 2024. *AI in Retail.* October 10. Accessed April 15, 2025. https://www.ibm.com/think/topics/ai-in-retail.

Epstein, Greg. 2024. *Silicon Valley's Obsession With AI Looks a Lot Like Religion.* November 22. Accessed April 21, 2025. https://thereader.mitpress.mit.edu/silicon-valleys-obsession-with-ai-looks-a-lot-like-religion/.

Ewing-Chow, Daphne. 2025. *The Latest AI Trends Transforming The Food Industry.* March 18. Accessed April 18, 2025.

https://www.forbes.com/sites/daphneewingchow/2025/03/18/these-are-the-latest-ai-trends-transforming-the-food-industry/.

Falcão, João Diogo, Carlos Ruiz, Adeola Bannis, Hae Young Noh, and Pei Zhang. 2021. "ISACS: In-Store Autonomous Checkout System for Retail." *Proceedings of the ACM on Interactive, Mobile, Wearable, and Ubiquitous Technologies* 5 (3): 1-26. Accessed April 15, 2025. doi:10.1145/3478086.

Ferreira, Fernando G.D.C., Amir H. Gandomi, and Rodrigo T.N. Cardoso. 2021. "Artificial Intelligence Applied to Stock Market Trading: A Review." *IEEE Access* 9: 30898-30917. Accessed April 17, 2025. doi:10.1109/ACESS.2021.30581.33.

Frye, Ma-Keba. 2025. *How Can AI Help You Grow Your Salon and Spa Business.* March 11. Accessed April 16, 2025. https://www.mindbodyonline.com/business/education/blog/what-ai-and-how-can-it-help-you-grow-your-salon-and-spa-business.

Geraghty, Tom. 2023. *The Swiss Cheese Model.* September 14. Accessed April 12, 2025. https://psychsafety.com/the-swiss-cheese-model/.

Gerken, Tom. 2024. *Bacon ice cream and nugget overload sees misfiring McDonald's AI withdrawn.* June 18. Accessed April 18, 2025. https://www.bbc.com/news/articles/c722gne7qngo.

Ghai, Neha. 2024. *Grocery Doppio AI Disruptors: 5 Tech Innovators Revolutionizing Autonomous Checkout Systems.* November 4. Accessed April 15, 2025. https://www.grocerydoppio.com/articles/ai-innovators-autonomous-checkout.

Ghazwani, Salman. 2021. "The Impact of AI-Enabled Checkouts on Shoppers' Attitudes ." Master Thesis, Auckland University of Technology, 1-118. Accessed April 15, 2025.

Gibbs, Alice. 2022. *Welcome to the First Ever McDonald's Where You're Served by Robots--In Texas.* December 24. Accessed April 18, 2025. https://www.newsweek.com/first-ever-mcdonalds-served-robots-texas-1769116.

Gonzalez, Eliezer. 2024. *Artificial Intelligence and Christianity.* January 14. Accessed April 20, 2025. https://goodnewsunlimited.com/artificial-intelligence-and-christianity/.

Gruchola, Malgorzata, Malgorzata Slawek-Czochra, and Robert Zielinski. 2024. "Artificial Intelligence as a Tool Supporting Prayer Practices." *Religions* 15 (3): 271. Accessed April 22, 2025. doi:10.3390/rel15030271.

Guinness, Emma. 2023. *Man creates robot that can cut hair automatically.* March 12. Accessed April 16, 2025. https://www.unilad.com/technology/man-creates-robot-cuts-hair-automatically-893468-20230312.

Harris, Mark. 2017. *Inside the First Church of Artificial Intelligence.* November 15. Accessed April 20, 2025. https://www.wired.com/story/anthony-levandowski-artificial-intelligence-religion/.

Hayes, Adam. 2025. *7 Unexpected Ways AI Can Transform Your Investment Strategy.* January 27. Accessed April 16, 2025. https://www.investopedia.com/using-ai-to-transform-investment-strategy-8778945#:~:text=Artificial%20intelligence%20(AI)%20has%20emerged,make%20more%20informed%20investment%20decisions.

Hossian, Fadeia. 2024. *Inclusive AI for people with disabilities: Key considerations.* December 3. Accessed April 12, 2025. https://www.cliffordchance.com/insights/resources/blogs/talking-tech/en/articles/2024/12/inclusive-ai-for-people-with-disabilities--key-considerations.html.

Howarth, Josh. 2025. *60+ Stats on AI Replacing Jobs.* April 3. Accessed April 12, 2025. https://explodingtopics.com/blog/ai-replacing-jobs.

Hubal, Nataliia. 2024. *Fuel Your Barbershop Growth with AI-Powered Client Insights.* Accessed April 16, 2025. https://help.barberly.com/en/articles/9486352-fuel-your-barbershop-growth-with-ai-powered-client-insights.

Huskey v. State Farm Fire & Casualty Company. 2023. 1:2022cv07014 (The United States District Court for the Northern District of Illinois Eastern Division, September 11). Accessed April 24, 2025.

Jackson, Aubriella. 2025. *2 dump truck drivers dead after head-on crash in Bedford County.* March 11.

Accessed April 12, 2025. https://www.wkrn.com/news/local-news/2-dump-truck-drivers-dead-after-head-on-crash-in-bedford-county/.

Jackson, Joshua Conrad, Kai Chi Yam, Pok Man Tang, Ting Liu, and Azim Shariff. 2023. "Exposure to Robot Preachers Undermines Religious Commitment." *Journal of Experimental Psychology: General* 152 (12): 3344-3358. Accessed April 21, 2025. doi:10.1037/xge0001443.

Jambrek, Stanko. 2024. "Christians Facing the Challenges of Artificial Intelligence." *KAIROS: Evangelical Journal of Theology* 18 (1): 75-94. Accessed April 20, 2025.

Jesuits ECE. 2024. *Religion Should Engage with Technology and AI.* September 2. Accessed April 21, 2025. https://jesuits.eu/news/2783-religion-should-engage-with-technology-and-ai.

Jingnan, Huo. 2024. *AI-generated images have become a new form of propaganda this election season.* October 18. Accessed April 22, 2025. https://www.npr.org/2024/10/18/nx-s1-5153741/ai-images-hurricanes-disasters-propaganda.

Johnson, Connor. 2019. *How has Technology and Artificial Intelligence Changed Christianity?* December 5. Accessed April 20, 2025. https://ncsureligion.wordpress.com/2019/12/05/how-has-technology-and-artificial-intelligence-changed-christianity/.

Joshi, Satyadhar. 2025. "Generative AI: Mitigating Workforce and Economic Disruptions While Strategizing Policy Responses for Governments and Companies." *International Journal of Advanced Research in Science, Communiction, and Technology* 5 (1): 480-486. Accessed April 12, 2025.

Kalman, David Zvi. 2024. *On AI, Jewish Thought Has Something Distinct to Say.* September 6. Accessed April 22, 2025. https://futureoflife.org/religion/ai-in-jewish-thought/.

Kami, Peter H. 2023. "Artificial Intelligence and the Future of Christianity: A Threat or Potential." *AKU: An African Journal of Contemporary Research* 4 (3): 83-93. Accessed April 22, 2025. doi:10.13140/RG.2.2.25435.54567 .

Kasyanau, Andrei. 2024. *How Artificial Intelligence Is Changing The Real Estate Market.* October 30.

Accessed April 20, 2025.
https://www.forbes.com/councils/forbestechcouncil/2024/10/30/how-artificial-intelligence-is-changing-the-real-estate-market/.

Kaya, Orçun, Jan Schildbach, Stefan Schneider, and Deutsche Bank Attorney General. 2019. "Artificial intelligence in banking." *Artificial intelligence* 1-9. Accessed April 17, 2025.

Kelly, Jack. 2025. *The Jobs That Will Fall First As AI Takes Over The Workplace.* April 25. Accessed April 29, 2025. https://www.forbes.com/sites/jackkelly/2025/04/25/the-jobs-that-will-fall-first-as-ai-takes-over-the-workplace/.

Korosec, Kirsten. 2021. *Anthony Levandowski closes his Church of AI.* February 18. Accessed April 21, 2025. https://techcrunch.com/2021/02/18/anthony-levandowski-closes-his-church-of-ai/?guccounter=1&guce_referrer=aHR0cHM6Ly93d3cuYmluZy5jb20v&guce_referrer_sig=AQAAAA7wdmg863gnmTB-zt3TzXLhI2FXY_yVFNL7TZTzFGnraTk6vg36gh2MeUfk6Bbt5qOnfLuRsCKSbhoFhRFjje7PEt--U1yZIA.

Krause, Reinhardt. 2025. *AI Stocks Face 'Show Me' Moment. Trump Tariffs Loom Over AI Models, Software.* April 16. Accessed April 16, 2025. https://www.investors.com/news/technology/artificial-intelligence-stocks/.

Kreps, Sarah, R. Miles McCain, and Miles Brundage. 2020. "All the News That's Fit to Fabricate: AI-Generated Text as a Tool of Media Misinformation." *Journal of Experimental Political Science* 9 (1): 104-117. Accessed April 18, 2025. doi:10.1017/XPS.2020.37.

Kumar, Indrajeet, Jyoti Rawat, Noor Mohd, and Shanawaz Husain. 2021. "Opportunities of Artificial Intelligence and Machine Learning in the Food Industry." *Journal of Food Quality* 2021 (1): 1-10. Accessed April 18, 2025. doi:10.1155/2021/4535567.

Kumar, Mahesh. 2022. "Optimized application of artificial intelligence (AI) in aviation market." *International Journal of Recent Research Aspects* 9 (4): 1-7. Accessed April 22, 2025.

Kumar, Naman, Jayant Dev Srivastava, and Harshit Bisht. 2019. "Artificial Intelligence in Insurance Sector." *Journal of the Gujarat Research Society* 21 (7): 79-91. Accessed April 16, 2025.

Kuo, Freddy. 2025. *Retail Theft Is Soaring--And AI Video Security Can Help.* April 10. Accessed April 15, 2025. https://www.forbes.com/councils/forbestechcouncil/2025/04/10/retail-theft-is-soaring-and-ai-video-security-can-help/.

Kuyenga, Madison C. Allen, Eleanor R. Glover Gladney, Michael Lachney, Marwin McKnight, Theordore S. Ransaw, Dominick Sanders, and Aman Yadav. 2023. *Barbershop Computing.* October 1. Accessed April 16, 2025. https://cacm.acm.org/opinion/barbershop-computing/.

Kyosuke, Futami, Tsutomu Terada, and Masahiko Tsukamoto. 2014. "A System for Supporting Self-Haircut Using Camera Equipped Robot." *Proceedings of the 12th International Conference on Advances in Mobile Computing and Multimedia* 34-42. Accessed April 16, 2025. doi:10.1145/2684103.2684143.

Lad, Sagar. 2025. *The Spiritual Side of AI: AI and Consciousness.* January 1. Accessed April 22, 2025. https://sagu94271.medium.com/the-spiritual-side-of-ai-ai-and-consciousness-237b1d374d1b.

Lapham, Jake. 2025. *Decoding Donald Trump's new official portrait.* January 17. Accessed April 22, 2025. https://www.bbc.com/news/articles/cy4mmrr7j8mo.

Lay-Flurrie, Jenny. 2025. *Microsoft Ability Summit 2025: Accessibiltiy in the AI era.* March 18. Accessed April 12, 2025. https://blogs.microsoft.com/blog/2025/03/18/microsoft-ability-summit-2025-accessibility-in-the-ai-era/.

Lecko, David. 2024. *The Complete Guide to AI in Real Estate.* October 1. Accessed April 20, 2025. https://www.dealmachine.com/blog/ai-real-estate.

Litvinova, Dasha, and Kostya Manendov. 2025. *What one Finnish church learned from creating a service almost entirely with AI.* March 8. Accessed April 20, 2025. https://apnews.com/article/finland-lutheran-church-artificial-intelligence-64135cc5e58578a89dcbaf0c227d9e3e.

Lucky, Kate. 2023. *AI Will Shape Your Soul.* October. Accessed April 20, 2025. https://www.christianitytoday.com/2023/09/artificial-intelligence-robots-soul-formation/.

Maher, Stephen. 2022. *What Happens When Human Truckers Are Replaced by AI? | Opinion.* February 3. Accessed April 15, 2025. https://www.newsweek.com/what-happens-when-human-truckers-are-replaced-ai-opinion-1675106.

Mahmoud, Ali B., Shehnaz Tehseen, and Leonora Fuxman. 2020. "The Dark Side of Artificial Intelligence in Retail Innovation." In *Retail Futures: The Good, the Bad, and the Ugly of the Digital Transformation*, edited by Eleonora Pantano, 165-180. Emerald Publishing Limited. Accessed April 15, 2025.

Mangrolia, Jayandrath R., Disha D. Panchal, and Keyur Patel. 2024. "The Role of Artificial Intelligence in Overcoming Disabilities: Challenges, Innovations, and Future Directions." *Cuestiones de Fisioterapia* 53 (1): 240-247. Accessed April 12, 2025.

Marotta, Deb. 2024. *Artificial Intelligence: How AI Is Changing Retail.* Accessed April 15, 2025. https://global.hitachi-solutions.com/blog/ai-in-retail/.

Matyszczyk, Chris. 2024. *Not always honest at supermarket self-checkout? AI is out to get you.* February 24. Accessed April 15, 2025. https://www.zdnet.com/article/not-always-honest-at-supermarket-self-checkout-ai-is-out-to-get-you/.

McBride, James. 2017. "Robotic Bodies and the Kairos of Humanoid Theologies." *Sophia* 58 (4): 663-676. Accessed April 21, 2025. doi:10.1007/s11841-017-0628-3.

Meghani, Manisha, and Hemlata Sinha. 2023. "Revolutionizing Retail: Design and Implementation." *International Journal on Recent and Innovation Trends in Computing and Communication* 11 (9): 4928-4933. Accessed April 15, 2025.

Minbiole, Anya. 2025. *More human-centered retail with AI.* April 10. Accessed April 15, 2025. https://www.microsoft.com/en-us/industry/blog/retail/2025/04/10/more-human-centered-retail-with-ai/.

Monti, Matteo. 2019. "Automated journalism and freedom of information: Ethical and juridical problems related to AI in the press field." *Opinio Juris in Comparatione,* 1: 1-17. Accessed April 19, 2025.

O'Brien, Keith, and Amanda Downie. 2024. *What is AI in banking?* May 1. Accessed April 16, 2025. https://www.ibm.com/think/topics/ai-in-banking.

—. 2024. *What is AI in insurance?* November 17. Accessed April 16, 2025. https://www.ibm.com/think/topics/ai-in-insurance#:~:text=AI%20in%20insurance%20is%20the,a%20large%20amount%20of%20data.

Oosthuizen, Kim. 2021. "Artificial Intelligence in Retail: The AI-Enabled Value Chain." Doctoral Dissertation, Stellenbosch University, 1-275. Accessed April 15, 2025. https://scholar.sun.ac.za/server/api/core/bitstreams/b259eac8-ae99-490f-b3eb-ab49aebe9aef/content.

Oyeniyi, Lawrence Damilare, Chinoyue Esther Ugochukwu, and Noluthando Zamanjomane Mhlongo. 2024. "Implementing AI in banking customer service: A review of current trends and future applications." *International Journal of Science and Research Archive* 11 (2): 1492-1509. Accessed April 16, 2025. doi:10.30574/ijsra.

Pachal, Pete. 2025. *The next big AI shift in media? Turning news into a 2-way conversation.* April 11. Accessed April 18, 2025. https://www.fastcompany.com/91314614/how-ai-is-transforming-news-into-a-two-way-conversation.

Patel, Ankit. 2024. *The Role of AI in Food Delivery Apps: Examples and Case Studies.* July 10. Accessed April 18, 2025. https://www.finextra.com/blogposting/26435/the-role-of-ai-in-food-delivery-apps-examples-and-case-studies.

Payne, Greg. 2024. *Drivers continue to struggle with warning system for low bridge.* August 29. Accessed April 121, 2025. https://www.fox29.com/news/drivers-continue-struggle-warning-system-low-bridge.

Pereira, Lester. 2025. *The Disruption of AI in Stock Markets: A New Era of Investment Decisions and Automation.* March 6. Accessed April 16, 2025. https://www.forbes.com/councils/forbestechcouncil/2025/03/06/the-disruption-of-ai-in-stock-markets-a-new-era-of-investment-decisions-and-automation/.

Pestano, Dana. 2024. *AI in Photography--The Good, The Bad, and the Ugly.* January 24. Accessed April 22, 2025. https://professionalphoto.online/ai-artificial-intelligence/ai-in-photography-the-good-the-bad-and-the-ugly/.

Pochechuev, Artem. 2025. *AI is improving accessibility for people with disabilities, but its impact depends on better data, inclusive design, and direct collaboration with the disability community.* Accessed April 12, 2025. https://swisscognitive.ch/2025/01/07/ai-for-disabilities-quick-overview-challenges-and-the-road-ahead/.

Posada, Julian, Nicholas Weller, and Wendy H. Wong. 2021. "We Haven't Gone Paperless Yet: Why the Printing Press Can Help Us Understand Data and AI." *Proceedings of the 2021 AAAI/ACM Conference on AI, Ethics, and Society* 864-872. Accessed April 19, 2025. doi:10.1145/3461702.3462604.

Prince, Nick. 2025. *Can I Use Ai as a Christian: Insights from Life Church's Technology Solutions Team.* April 10. Accessed April 20, 2025. https://finds.life.church/ai-as-a-christian-in-ministry/.

Puttaparthi, Murali. 2025. *AI in Real Estate: Use Cases, Implementation Challenges and Looking Ahead.* Accessed April 20, 2025. https://ablypro.com/ai-in-real-estate.

Puzio, Anna. 2023. "Robot, let us pray! Can and should robots have religious functions? An ethical exploration of religious robots." *AI & Society* 40: 1019-1035. Accessed April 20, 2025. doi:10.1007/s00146-023-01812-z.

Rahmani, Amir Masoud, Bahareh Rezazadeh, Majid Haghparast, Wei-Che Chang, and Shen Guan Ting. 2023. "Applications of Artificial Intelligence in the Economy, Including Applications in Stock Trading, Market Analysis, and Risk Management." *IEEE Access* 11: 80769-80793. Accessed April 16, 2025. doi:10.1109/ACCESS.2023.3300036.

Rao, Natasha L., Nicholas T. Badalamenti, and Nicole E. Wilinski. 2024. *Artificial intelligence and the insurance industry.* December. Accessed April 16, 2025. https://www.michbar.org/journal/Details/Artificial-intelligence-and-the-insurance-industry?ArticleID=4986.

Rasouli, Mohammad, Ravi Chiruvolu, and Ali Risheh. 2023. "AI for Investment: A Platorm

Disruption." *arXiv preprint arXiv:2311.06251* 1-9. Accessed April 16, 2025.

Reed, Jeff. 2022. *4 Ways Your Church Can Use Tesla's New Humanoid Robot.* November 28. Accessed April 20, 2025. https://exponential.org/4-ways-your-church-can-use-teslas-new-humanoid-robot/.

Rigner, Anton. 2019. "AI-based machine vision for retail." Master Thesis, Lund University, 1-34. Accessed April 15, 2025. https://lup.lub.lu.se/luur/download?func=downloadFile&recordOId=8985308&fileOId=8985340.

Rossini, Peter. 2000. "Using Expert Systems and Artificial Intelligence for Real Estate Forecasting." *Sixth Annual Pacific-Rim Real Estate Society Conference* 1-10. Accessed April 20, 2025.

Rothman, Joshua. 2025. *Will A.I. Save The News?* April 8. Accessed April 18, 2025. https://www.newyorker.com/culture/open-questions/will-ai-save-the-news.

Ryan, Dustin. 2024. *A Christian's Perspective on Artificial Intelligence.* May 6. Accessed April 20, 2025. https://christoverall.com/article/longform/a-christians-perspective-on-artificial-intelligence/.

Sachani, Dipakkumar Kanubhai, Niravkumar Dhameliya, Kishore Mullangi, Sunil Kumar Reddy Anumandla, and Sai Charan Reddy Vennapusa. 2021. "Enhancing Food Service Sales through AI and." *Global Disclosure of Economics and Business* 10 (2): 105-116. Accessed April 18, 2025. doi:10.18034/gdeb.v10i2.754.

Sahota, Neil. 2024. *AI In The Culinary World: Revolutionizing Restaurant Ops & Customer Experience.* March 13. Accessed April 18, 2025. https://www.forbes.com/sites/neilsahota/2024/03/13/ai-in-the-culinary-world-revolutionizing-restaurant-ops--customer-experience/.

—. 2024. *Navigating The Skies With AI: How Arlines Are Transforming Air Travel.* March 29. Accessed April 22, 2025. https://www.forbes.com/sites/neilsahota/2024/03/29/navigating-the-skies-with-ai-how-airlines-are-transforming-air-travel/.

Salvemini, Chris. 2024. *TDOT: Jackknifed semi-truck blocks I-40 East near Rockwood in Roane County.*

January 19. Accessed April 12, 2025. https://www.wbir.com/article/traffic/roane-county-crash-i-40-east-january-18-2024/51-e36b172a-1aef-405e-a98b-81e640d8674b.

Sepenu, Alexander K., and Linda Eliasen. 2022. "A Machine Learning Approach to Revenue Generation within the Professional Hair Care Industry." *SMU Data Science Review* 6 (1): 1-28. Accessed April 16, 2025. https://scholar.smu.edu/datasciencereview/vol6/iss1/6.

Sheth, Jagdish N., Varsha Jain, Gourav Roy, and Amrita Chakraborty. 2022. " AI-driven banking services: the next frontier for a personalized experience in the emerging market." *International Journal of Bank Marketing* 40 (6): 1248-1271. Accessed April 16, 2025. doi:10.1108/IJBM-09-2021-0449.

Simpson, Carissa. 2023. *Largest Buc-cee's in country opens in Sevierville.* June 26. Accessed April 12, 2025. https://www.wvlt.tv/2023/06/26/largest-buc-ees-country-opens-sevierville/.

Skinner, Andy. 2023. *Artificial intelligence in beauty salons.* April 10. Accessed April 16, 2025. https://easyweek.io/artificial-intelligence-in-beauty-industry.html.

Sloan, Nick. 2024. *Driverless semi-truck rolls through Lawrence residential area, comes to rest between two homes.* July 25. Accessed April 12, 2025. https://www.kmbc.com/article/driverless-semi-truck-rolls-through-lawrence-kansas-residential/61703544.

Sneed, Calvin. 2015. *"Stumbling Out of the Fog: "Memories Of The Worst Traffic Accident in Tennessee History.* December 11. Accessed April 12, 2025. https://newschannel9.com/news/local/stumbling-out-of-the-fog-memories-of-the-worst-traffic-accident-in-tennessee-history.

Spencer, Amanda. 2024. *Artificial Intelligence in Retail: 6 Use Cases and Examples.* April 19. Accessed April 15, 2025. https://www.forbes.com/sites/sap/2024/04/19/artificial-intelligence-in-retail-6-use-cases-and-examples/.

Square. 2024. *Artificial Intelligence is Ready for its Close-up at Spas and Salons.* October 29. Accessed April 16, 2025. https://squareup.com/us/en/the-bottom-line/operating-your-business/ai-beauty-industry.

Stoffers, Carl. 2024. *Self-Service Kiosks Are Changing Fast Food--But Not Without Unexpected*

Consequences. September 27. Accessed April 18, 2025.
https://www.entrepreneur.com/franchises/the-unintended-consequences-of-fast-food-ordering-kiosks/480269.

Straut, Nicholas. 2024. *How To Use AI To Make Money.* July 25. Accessed April 16, 2025.
https://www.forbes.com/sites/investor-hub/article/how-to-use-ai-to-make-money-investing/.

The Church of Jesus Christ of Latter-Day Saints. 2024. *Guiding Principles for the Church of Jesus Christ's Use of Artificial Intelligence.* March 13. Accessed April 22, 2025.
https://newsroom.churchofjesuschrist.org/article/church-jesus-christ-artificial-intelligence.

2023. "The Evolution of AI on the Commercial Flight Deck: Finding Balance Between Efficiency and Safety While Maintaining the Integrity of Operator Trust." *Artificial Intelligence, Social Computing and Wearable Technologies* 13: 14. Accessed April 22, 2025.
doi:10.54941/ahfe1004175.

Torres, Allen Jasfer G., Catherine Ann D. Pilapil, Mathew L. Flores, Criselle J. Centeno, Gaypelyn M. Casiw, and Mary Grace D. Nulud. 2024. "Lash Tech: A Web App-Based Lash Recommendation, Virtual Try-On, and Seamless Booking App Using Geo Location Powered by Artificial Intelligence." *Journal of Electrical Systems* 20 (5s): 1118-1125. Accessed April 16, 2025.

Tsirulnik, Yevgeni. 2025. *The Future of Self-Checkout: Harnessing AI and Automation for Smarter Security.* March 18. Accessed April 15, 2025.
https://www.forbes.com/councils/forbestechcouncil/2025/03/18/the-future-of-self-checkout-harnessing-ai-and-automation-for-smarter-security/.

Türkal, Baris. 2024. *The impact of Artificial Intelligence on Barbering.* February 7. Accessed April 18, 2025. https://barbersets.com/blogs/blogs/the-impact-of-artificial-intelligence-on-barbering?srsltid=AfmBOorBTLu4JfZnKrAANnZwWflaoIgX1cn8eMNy-truUEGO4_XjEjaT.

U.S. Bureau of Labor Statistics. 2025. *AI impacts in BLS employment projections.* March 11. Accessed

April 11, 2025. https://www.bls.gov/opub/ted/2025/ai-impacts-in-bls-employment-projections.htm.

Vesala, Juha. 2022. "Press publishers right and artificial intelligence." *Artificial Intelligence and the Media* (Edward Elgar Publishing) 240-271. Accessed April 18, 2025. doi:10.4337/9781839109973.

Walters, Holly. 2023. *Robots are performing Hindu rituals. Some worshippers fear they'll be replaced.* March 11. Accessed April 22, 2025. https://www.pbs.org/newshour/world/robots-are-performing-hindu-rituals-some-worshippers-fear-theyll-be-replaced.

Walton, Abbey. 2023. *Photos: 1 dead after tractor-trailer strikes Jasper home Wednesday.* July 27. Accessed April 12, 2025. https://newschannel9.com/news/local/1-dead-after-tractor-trailer-strikes-jasper-home-wednesday-night-marion-county-tennessee.

WBBJ 7 Eyewitness News. 2025. *FedEx truck catches fire after crashing on I-40.* March 25. Accessed April 12, 2025. https://www.wbbjtv.com/2025/03/25/fedex-truck-catches-fire-after-crashing-on-i-40/.

Wibowo, Gandi, and Stephanas Budiono. 2024. "The Relationship Between the Church and Humanoid Robots in the Posthumanism Era." *KnE Social Sciences* 265-274. Accessed April 22, 2025. doi: 10.18502/kss.v9i22.16726.

Yoo, Uksang, Nathaniel Dennler, Eliot Xing, Maja Mataric, Stefanos Nikolaidis, Jeffrey Ichbnowski, and Jean Oh. 2025. "Soft and Compliant Contact-Rich Hair Manipulation and Care." *arXiv preprint arXiv:2501.02630* 1-12. Accessed April 16, 2025.

Zarfis, Alex, Christopher P. Holland, and Alistair Milne. 2019. "Evaluating the impact of AI on insurance: The four emerging AI- and data-driven business models." *Emerald Open Research* 1 (1): 1-19. Accessed April 16, 2025. doi:10.35241/emeraldopenres.13249.1.

Zheng, Yutong. 2024. "Buddhist Transformation in the Digital Age: AI (Artificial Intelligence) and Humanistic Buddhism." *Religions* 15 (1): 79. Accessed April 22, 2025. doi:10.3390/rel15010079.

ABOUT THE AUTHOR

Elysia Duke, a native of northwestern Tennessee, is a prolific writer on the autism spectrum. She began her writing career in college and one of her English composition papers on the topic of virtual reality and autism was nominated for a writing conference. She holds a Bachelor of Science Degree in Political Science from the University of Tennessee at Martin, Master of Public Administration degree from Murray State University in Kentucky, and a Master of Business Administration degree from the University of Tennessee at Martin.

She is passionate about the political world and wanted to do something to change the political arena along with social justice. She previously published "How AI Would Destroy Humanity." This book is the first added to her political repertoire. Her second book, "ADA Compliance: What Is Going On?" is her second. Her mantra is, "the war isn't over yet, and it'll never be" meaning the continuation to fight for disability rights.